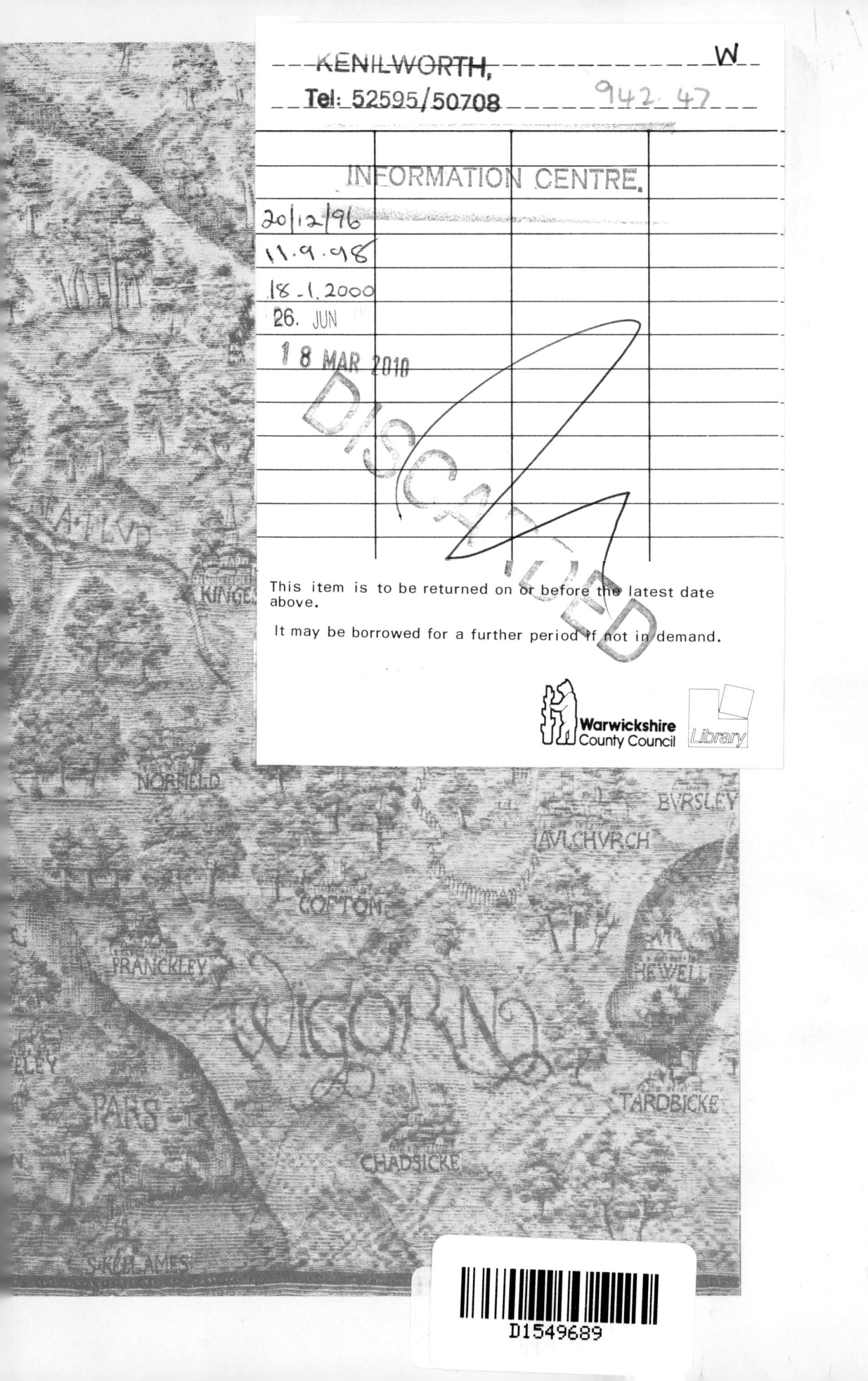

THE BOOK OF REDDITCH

FRONT COVER: A prospect of Redditch in 1877. Engraving by W.T.
Heming from *The Needle Region and its resources*, (1877).

Coat of Arms of the Borough of Redditch.

THE BOOK OF REDDITCH

BY

RALPH RICHARDSON

BARRACUDA BOOKS LIMITED
BUCKINGHAM, ENGLAND
MCMLXXXVI

PUBLISHED BY BARRACUDA BOOKS LIMITED
BUCKINGHAM, ENGLAND
AND PRINTED BY
HOLYWELL PRESS LIMITED
OXFORD, ENGLAND

BOUND BY STANDARD BOOKBINDING CO. LTD.
LONDON, ENGLAND

JACKET PRINTED BY
CHENEY & SONS LIMITED
BANBURY, OXON

LITHOGRAPHY BY
MRM GRAPHICS LIMITED
WINSLOW, ENGLAND

TEXT SET IN BASKERVILLE BY
CREATIVE SERVICES
AYLESBURY, ENGLAND

ISBN 0 86023 261 1

Contents

Acknowledgements

The production of this book has only been possible with the help and encouragement of many people.

I am particularly indebted to the Staff of Redditch Library and especially Mr Brian Hart, the Assistant County Librarian, and Mr Philip Davis, whose responsibilities include looking after the excellent Local History collection. I have learned a great deal from Mr Robin Whittaker in his University Extra-Mural classes at the County Record Office, St Helen's, Worcester.

I am very grateful to a former librarian of Redditch, Mr Roy Vann, who many years ago awoke my interest in the local history of my adopted town. He has read the manuscript of the book and made valuable criticisms which prevented my making errors. Any mistakes which have crept through are my responsibility, not his.

The maps and plans were produced by Mr Martin Richardson, with the help of the Surveying Science Department of the University of Newcastle-upon-Tyne.

Rev Stanley Rose, Superintendent Methodist Minister for Redditch, drew my attention to the early beginnings of Methodism in the area.

I am indebted to many people for help with finding, and for permission to reproduce, illustrations. My thanks go particularly to Redditch Library; the Public Record Office; the Victoria and Albert Museum; the *Redditch Advertiser/Indicator;* Rev John Cook, Vicar of Beoley; Rev David Bosworth, Minister of Headless Cross Methodist Church; Mr Jeremy Barker; Mr Michael Wojczynski; Mr David Brazier of Linden Studios, and lastly, but by no means least, Mr Melvyn Amos for the loan of many of his early 20th century Redditch post cards.

My indebtedness to all those who have written previously about the Redditch area is, I hope, evident in the bibliography at the end. Numerous others have contributed ideas and encouragement over the years, not least the members of The Redditch Society. This book grew out of a lecture given to them.

It is traditional to thank one's wife. I had not realised until starting this enterprise how vital her support and patience would be.

Redditch 1986   Ralph Richardson

Dedication

For Joan and Martin

Foreword

Councillor Arthur Price, Mayor of Redditch 1986

Redditch is located south of Birmingham on the A441, with its town centre perched on a hill, and the spire of St Stephen's as the main landmark. So it was known by the vast majority of people who did not reside here prior to the middle sixties. If prompted, the more knowledgeable would exclaim: 'Ah! yes, needles and the fishing tackle industry'. In fact, from the beginning of this century, Redditch was the home of many other metal-based industries.

From the mid-sixties, with the designation of New Town status in 1964, industrial diversification accelerated. It is appropriate that, with the conclusion of the main plan, the author of this book, Ralph Richardson, should remind us that Redditch is not so new but, in fact, has a long and interesting history. Ralph's profound interest in the heritage of the town, supplemented by his academic capabilities, has enabled him to produce a comprehensive and readable book. In his role as Headmaster of one of the town's largest High Schools he has the opportunity to instil civic pride in the young people in his care and make them aware of their responsibilities to their heritage.

Preface

by Roy Vann ALA, former Chief Librarian, Redditch

Since I first came to Redditch in 1939, I have found much public interest in the history of the town and its environs. The resources to satisfy this interest have long existed in the very extensive collection in the Public Library.

However, we have had to wait till now for a good book on the subject. Ralph Richardson's account is well written, authoritative and always interesting. It is a very good introduction to the subject for the general reader.

'A considerable manufacture . . . .' (Nash) demonstrated by Heming in 1877.

In Other Words

In this parish of Tardebigge is the hamlet or chapelry of REDDITCH, where is a considerable manufacture of needles: about 400 persons are employed here, and in the neighbourhood above 2000.

T. Nash: *History and Antiquities of Worcestershire* (1782)

Never was an habitation more thoroughly odious — red soil, mince-pie woods, and black and greasy needleworkers.

Water Savage Landor, 1830

Redditch is well supplied with schools, only two other places in the county exceeding it in this respect, and they are comparatively well conducted, two are more especially so . . . There is above the average proportion of crime from this town, but only one female, and from the lightness of the sentences, the crimes could not have been serious. The prisoners were almost entirely uneducated, and badly connected, but their wages were considerably above the average, and there are above the proportion of public houses in the town.

Bentley's *Ancient and Modern History of Worcestershire* (c1840)

This enterprising town — the principal seat of the needle trade — wears the aspect of rapid progression . . . I found its streets as bustling as the county town, its artizans everywhere tidily dressed, the shops sparkling and redundant and all things betokening comfort if not luxury . . . the inhabitants of Redditch are a God-fearing people.

John Noake: *The Rambler* Vol II (1851)

Needles cost human life, too, at a terrible rate. It never was true, as it is often said to have been, that needlemakers rarely lived beyond thirty years of age: but it was, for a long time, true that every needle that was pointed helped to shorten some man's life . . . The pointers died of consumption in a few years. If boys tried the work, they were gone before twenty.

Charles Dickens: *Household Words* (1852)

The erection of dwelling-houses has of late proceeded briskly: new streets have sprung up in all directions.

History, Topography and Directory of Worcestershire (1860)

Redditch, which stands as metropolis to this district, is a very clean and beautiful little town in Worcestershire . . . Nothing in the distant view of it, as it lies on the slopes of a gentle elevation, would give the impression that it has made itself remarkable as the centre of an important industry.

Alexander Hay Japp: *Industrial Curiosities* (1877)

I was born at a very early period of my life, of poor but respectable parents, in the small and unfrequented village of Redditch. Though present at the event, I cannot exactly fix the date, but I may say I came in with the nineteenth century.

William Avery, first historian of Redditch: 1887

Now good night, darling, and if you do dream about needles be sure you dream about William Bartleet and Sons' Archer Brand . . .

Edgar R.S. Bartleet: *History of a Needle*

It is one of the reddest towns I have ever seen.

L.T.C. Rolt: *Worcestershire* (1949)

. . . the decision to create here a new town has caused considerable misgiving.

Arthur Mee: *The King's England — Worcestershire* (1968)

The finest place in England to live, work and play.

Chairman of the Redditch Development Corporation.

LEFT: Her Majesty Queen Elizabeth II arriving in Redditch for her visit on 5 July 1983. RIGHT: The Queen inaugurates the National Needle Museum on 5 July and BELOW: signs her portrait, given to the Redditch Development Corporation that same day; now in the Redditch Library. (Photographs by courtesy of the *Redditch Advertiser/Indicator*)

New Town, Old Town

Redditch is today a large and thriving New Town, some fifteen miles south of Birmingham, set in the attractive rolling countryside of north-east Worcestershire. Its dramatic new roads, its high-technology factories and its magnificent space-age Kingfisher shopping centre give it an air of having only just arrived. In only 20 years it has become the second largest town in the new county of Hereford and Worcester. Particularly when seen at night from Gorcott Hill, its size surprises all who see it. At first glance it does not appear to have a history. If it ever did, the bulldozers and the developers buried it during the past two decades.

Compared with its near neighbours, Warwick, Stratford, Alcester, Evesham and Worcester, there is apparently little to see. The Ordnance Survey map, however, shows a Roman road going straight through Redditch, with another not far away. The map's laconic reference to *Site of Abbey* disguises the finest archaeological monastic site in England, with sufficient excavation to keep the experts happy until well into the next century. One of the surviving water mills on the River Arrow has been preserved to become the National Needle Museum. Opened by Her Majesty the Queen in July 1983, the Forge Mill Museum is a testimony to a town which, for well over a century, has been synonymous with the making of needles.

While the Parish Church of Redditch is a mere stripling of one hundred and thirty years, there are two mediaeval churches within what may be loosely described as Redditch. One was mentioned in Domesday, and still has its eighteenth century oil lighting. The other has a collection of monuments to the Sheldon family which are of national importance.

Many of the people born and bred in what they term *Old Redditch* know that the town has had a fascinating history since the Industrial Revolution. The many newcomers to Redditch may be forgiven for thinking the town had no past. Until recently there has been no published work on the history of Redditch. The needle industry has been more than secretive about its past. Yet the beautiful landscape of the Arrow Valley and its surrounding hills have a history stretching back more than two thousand years.

It is the aim of this book to tell the story of those two millenia. Redditch requires exploration if it is to be understood. It also needs people who care about its preservation. Its name is known world-wide because it appeared on every one of the millions of packets of needles which have been exported to every corner of the globe. Yet the town has lacked — and still lacks —a sense of civic pride. There is so much in Redditch of which to be proud. A former Chairman of Redditch Development Corporation claimed that Redditch would be 'the finest place in the Midlands to live, work and play'. His dream may be nearer realisation if we realise how fascinating is its past.

LEFT: St Stephen's Church, engraved by W.T. Heming, c1870. RIGHT: The Gatehouse Chapel of St Stephen, Bordesley Abbey, c1805. BELOW: Redditch Market, 1910.

Valley of the Arrow

For most towns the prehistoric period is buried under two thousand years of subsequent building, and its discovery depends upon archaeological investigation, usually preceding redevelopment. All towns have a prehistoric period if only it can be found. Redditch did not exist before the 13th century, and its prehistory is therefore much longer than that of most towns. There is no written evidence for settlement in what is now central Redditch, before a monk of Bordesley Abbey referred to *Rubeo Fossato* in 1200. He appears to have tried to translate the English words Red Ditch into something akin to Latin, and this is the first mention we have of a settlement in the area we understand as Redditch. Prior to this we are forced to rely upon artefacts and the landscape for hints about man's settling here. The sad fact is that there is scarcely a shred of evidence to suggest that anyone lived in Redditch before the Cistercian monks arrived in 1138.

A few prehistoric flints have been found during the Bordesley Abbey excavations of recent years, but in insufficient quantitites to prove that a community lived there. For the rest of the Redditch area, there is nothing — no axeheads, no worked flints, no antler picks, no burial mounds, no hill forts: if Redditch was to be typical of the rest of England, we should have to assume that the Romans occupied a deserted land. It is, of course, hardly surprising that the prehistoric settlers of Britain steered well clear of the Arrow Valley. Any present-day gardener in Redditch will provide the reason — the sticky clay which makes cultivation in the area so difficult. Present-day Redditch town centre is built on the spur of a ridge of high ground running roughly north-south, from the Birmingham Plateau to the edge of the Vale of Evesham. There are bands of sand on this ridge but, for the most part, the soil is a heavy red clay. It was once used for brick-making, and nineteenth century Redditch was once described as a very red town with most of its buildings of local brick. Down in the valley of the meandering River Arrow there were no patches of sand to lighten the clay: the flattish valley, a few miles wide, must have been even less inviting for cultivation than it is today. It has been suggested that the Arrow was a much larger river than the mere stream which flows gently along the valley today. It may even have been a series of shallow pools and marshes, such as exist today at Ipsley Alders. So ill-drained and heavy a clay soil had no attractions for the waves of invaders of pre-Roman times, and north eastern Worcestershire has revealed so little evidence of man's activities that it is safe to assume that the land was empty. Like so much of lowland Britain it was covered in trees — oaks, ashes, elms and alders. It must have looked impenetrable.

None of this original greenwood survives in the Redditch area. Indeed, throughout the whole of Britain there are but a handful of patches of woodland which the experts can, with any certainty, describe as natural wild-wood. It is not difficult, however, to imagine what this woodland looked like. Redditch is lucky to have preserved a number of wooded areas, the most extensive of which is Pitcher Oak Wood, a little over half a mile from the town centre. Though occasionally subject to the attention of forestry workers, these woods are largely natural, with substantial oak trees growing out of a tangle of brambles and other bushes. While the pathways are clear, it is difficult to force one's way through the undergrowth. The clay soil beneath is heavy and waterlogged in winter and

15

exceedingly hard in summer. If prehistoric man, with his stone axes and antler picks, ever came in this direction he would have found the prospect of clearing and cultivating the area much too daunting.

There was pre-Roman settlement in Worcestershire. There is evidence of man on the fertile river terraces of the Severn and the Avon. Defensible hill forts, which were probably used as refuges for both cattle and tribesmen in times of danger, are still clearly to be seen on Bredon Hill south of Evesham, on Wychbury Hill above Stourbridge, and on Woodbury Hill at Great Witley but not in the Redditch area. Though modern research suggests that Neolithic man was much more energetic in clearing woodland and establishing farms with recognisable boundaries than used to be thought, there is no evidence for this in our area. Until the arrival of the Romans, the signs that any man came near this corner of present-day Worcestershire are slight.

The name of the small river, which flows southwards from the Lickey Hills through the wide valley until it joins forces with the Alne before joining the Avon, may be pre-Roman. *Arrow* is an unusual name for a river: the only other English Arrow is in neighbouring Herefordshire, though there is one in Ireland. Natural features such as rivers and hills often retain pre-Roman or Celtic names. It is not clear, however, that *Arrow* is Celtic; historians of place names do not pretend to know its meaning, but they do suggest that the river was named before the Saxons came, for they were the people who named almost all the settlements in the area. It is just possible that the Saxon tribe which first settled the Valley in the 9th century AD met a British settler and learned from him the name of the river — but such a supposition can hardly be regarded as historical evidence for pre-Roman settlement here.

Two other early place names which have attracted the attention of the historians are the Ridge Way and the Port Way. The former is still used for the road south from Headless Cross, which clings to the summit of the not inconsiderable ridge which is the western edge of the Arrow Valley. The Port Way refers to the road along the dry tops of the Arrow Valley's eastern side, again running roughly north-south. It has been suggested that both these roads were once prehistoric trackways, which survived into the mediaeval period, when they gained their present-day names. If so, it is possible to imagine Neolithic, Bronze or Iron Age men, who had something to sell or barter, walking along these ridge ways, glad to keep feet reasonably dry, feeling secure because of the good views both tracks commanded, and perhaps being grateful that they did not have to penetrate the marshy, wooded valley below.

There is little here in two track ways and a river to suggest that anyone had ventured to settle in the Arrow Valley. However, all this certainty was thrown into doubt in 1969 when the Redditch Development Corporation was engaged in preliminary work for the building of the New Town. An excavator driver, working on the banks of the River Arrow, unearthed a massive tree trunk. The log was of oak some 25 feet long. What excited the press, and others, was that the log was pointed at both ends and looked remarkably like a dug-out canoe. In the centre, its cross-section was D-shaped, and there appeared to be a hollow in the middle where paddlers might sit or perhaps store something. A week later a second, though smaller, log was discovered. Great care was taken to prevent the saturated, but well preserved, timbers from drying out too quickly. Well protected, they were taken to the Worcestershire County Museum at Hartlebury for investigation. The press described them as dug-out canoes; the larger one became known as the Ipsley Canoe, since it had been found in the parish of Ipsley. It was easy to weave a story to explain their being found on the banks of a river.

The River Arrow, today a small river, had clearly been much wider in prehistoric times. Perhaps the Arrow Valley had had a series of shallow meres, or perhaps been filled by a substantial lake. Such an area would have attracted quantities of wildfowl, which early man would have found desirable for the pot. The canoe was clearly a type of punt, used for hunting duck. One man, armed with spear or bow and arrow, stood or lay on the flattened prow. His partner either sat in the middle quietly paddling, or stood on the flat stern armed with a punting pole. For some reason the crew of

16

the Ipsley Canoe beached their craft, pulling it up on the bank and perhaps covering it with grass, reeds and branches. They never returned. A variety of dates was suggested for the boat. The most exciting theory was that the Ipsley Canoe was Mesolithic, some 17,000 years old, and the earliest boat ever to be discovered in the British Isles, the companion for the Mesolithic paddle found in Yorkshire. Had this been true, the Ipsley Canoe would have had pride of place in the National Maritime Museum at Greenwich.

Unfortunately, the Hartlebury experts soon ended speculation. Carbon dating showed the log to date from about 760 BC. Far from being Mesolithic, it dated from the late Bronze Age. If it was a canoe, it was extremely primitive for its date. Worse still, there were no toolmarks of any kind. The experts concluded that it was nothing more than an oddly shaped oak trunk, preserved in the saturated clay and silt of the river bank. What had seemed to be the most exciting evidence for early settlement in the Arrow Valley had evaporated to nought. It will, however be a long time before those newspaper stories and the early theories are forgotten, and the story of the primitive hunters of the region is likely to become an indelible piece of Redditch folk lore. Volume II of *The Archaeology of Redditch New Town* ought to disillusion even the most romantic.

There is one other feature in the landscape of Redditch which merits investigation in seeking for early settlement here. Just to the south of Beoley Church, across the B4101, and at a height of 450 feet above sea level, the Ordnance Survey map has an earthwork marked in Gothic script *The Mount*. This appears to be a defended encampment some 1¼ acres in extent, with massive ditches and ramparts. Like all hill forts it has extensive views from its flat interior. Though the defensive ditches are not found on the northern side and though the much later digging of marl has changed its shape, The Mount could well have been a small hill fort of the Iron Age period. It is much smaller than those elsewhere. The traditional view, supported by Dr Treadway Nash in his *History and Antiquities of Worcestershire*,(1781/2) is that there was a castle here, though there is no documentary evidence to support the theory. The Beauchamp family, mediaeval lords of the manor of Beoley, had a hunting lodge in the 13th century and The Mount seems the probable site of this long vanished building. But before the Beauchamps arrived, Beoley had belonged to the Saxon Abbey of Pershore. In the Great Charter of King Edgar, confirming the Abbey's estates, there is reference to a *Burghleahe* or camp-clearing at Beoley. This word usually refers to pre-Saxon camps. The Beoley Camp is certainly not Roman. It is just possible that it is a prehistoric defended site. If so it is the only evidence we have that anyone lived in the Arrow Valley before the Roman invasions. It may thus be the earliest example of New Town Development.

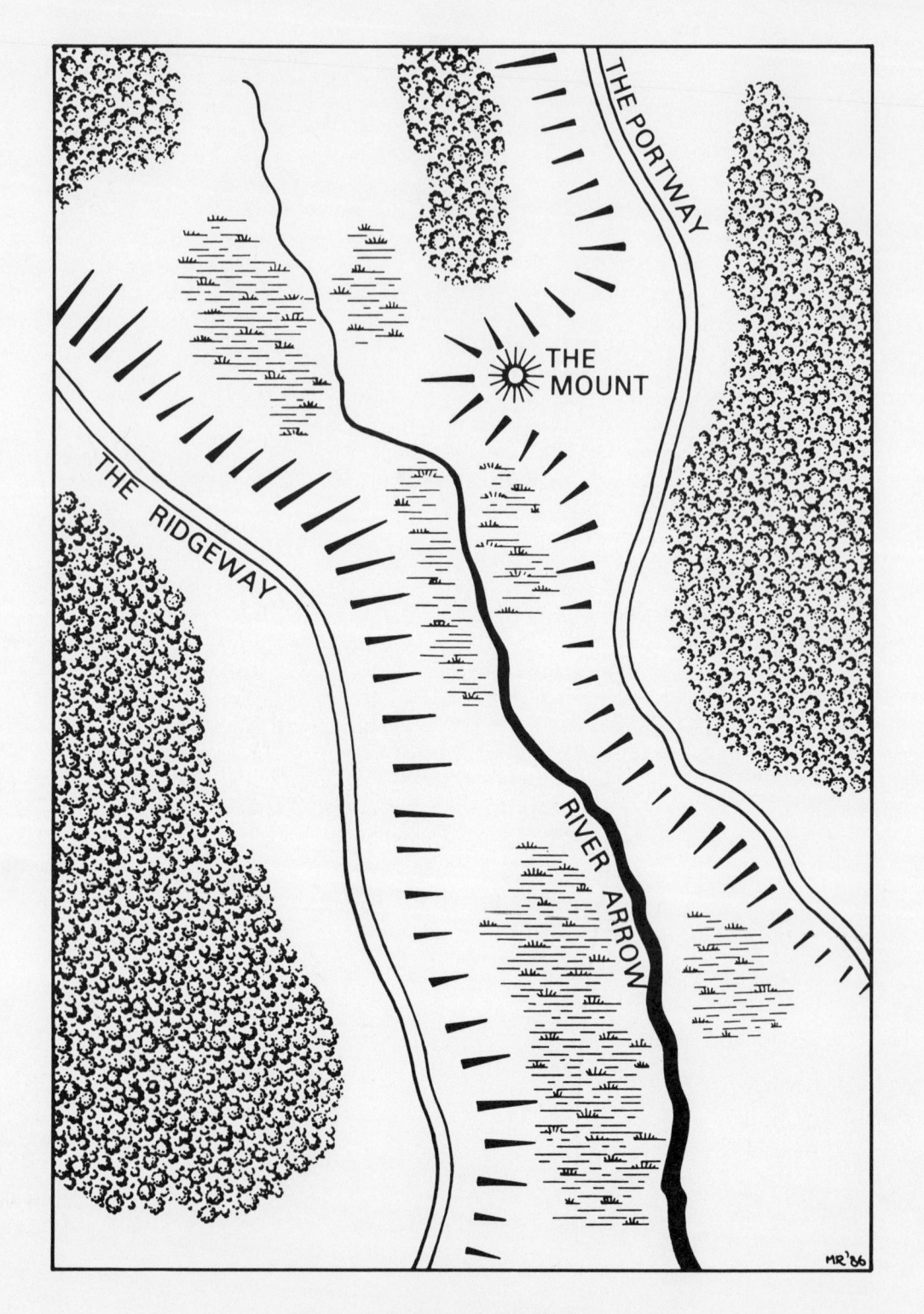

The Arrow Valley in prehistoric times.

ABOVE: The Arrow Valley. BELOW: The Mount, Beoley — probably a
prehistoric hill-fort.

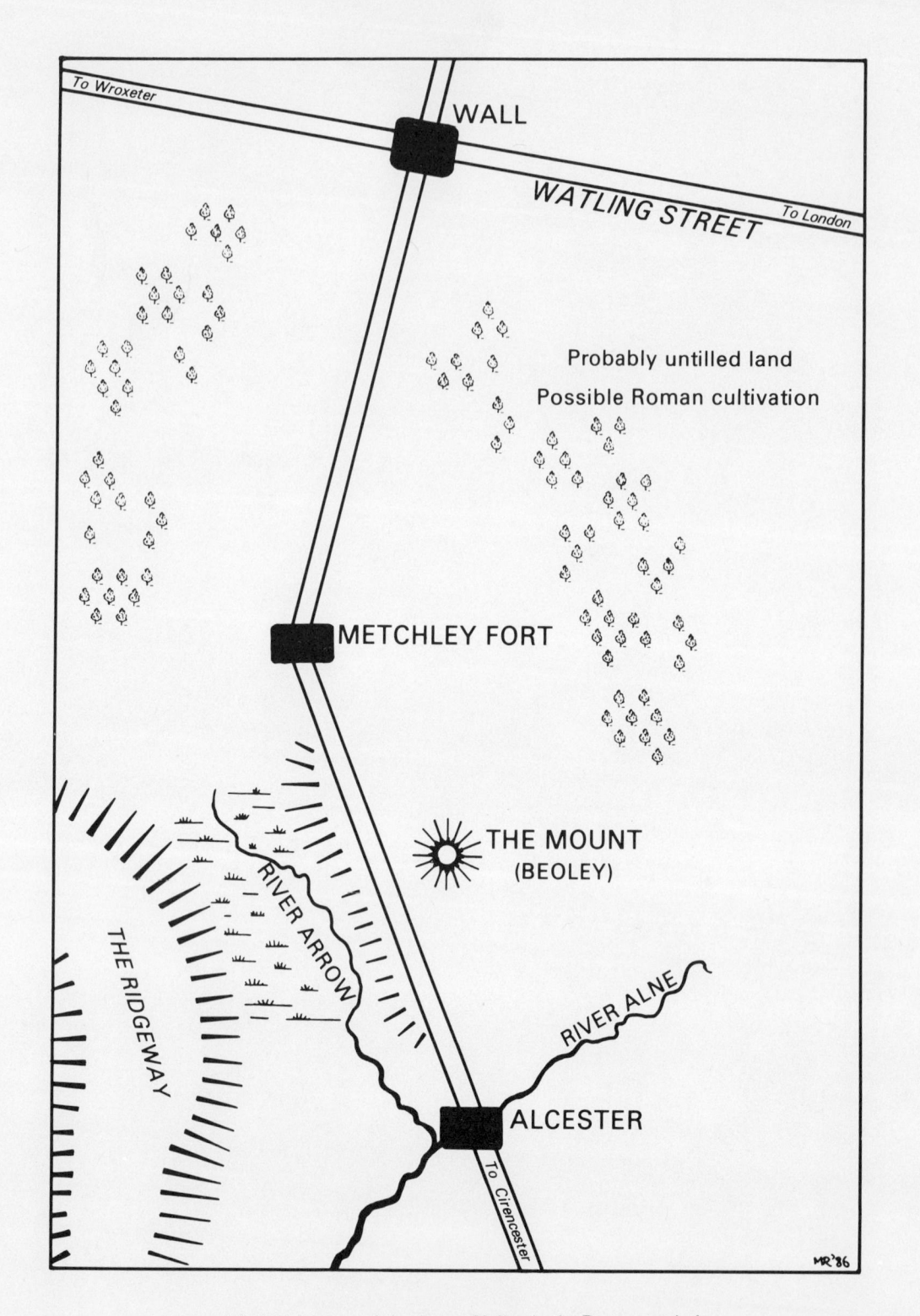

Icknield Street and the Arrow Valley in the Roman period.

Invaders and Settlers

Although Julius Caesar made two raids on Britain in 55 and 54 BC, the invasion and conquest of the island was not begun until AD 43, when the Emperor Claudius decided to add new territory to his Empire and glory to his name. Claudius and his successors established a Roman presence in the south-east, and three legions were despatched from Colchester to bring Britain into the Roman Empire. By AD 79 the frontier was a string of Roman forts from Lincoln in the north to Exeter in the south west. They were connected by a military road, now known as the Fosse Way. Though this did not remain a frontier for long, it was only the area south east of the Fosse Way which became truly Romanised. Lands beyond the Fosse Way were never governed by civilians, but remained under military jurisdiction. Our area fell under the Roman army's administration.

The Romans found the Arrow Valley as uninviting as everyone else. But they did build a road across our region. This came off Watling Street at Wall *(Letocetum)* near Lichfield and ran as far as the Cotswolds, where it joined the Fosse Way to Cirencester *(Corinium)*. It can be seen as mounds across Sutton Park, north of Birmingham, and its course south of the city can easily be traced on the Ordnance Survey map. It ran from Metchley Fort, in the grounds of the University of Birmingham, by way of Kings Norton, Weatheroak Hill, below Beoley Church to Studley, Alcester, Bidford on Avon and beyond. Much of its course remains as a metalled road and it is still the most convenient route from the Redditch area to the picturesque Cotswolds.

It did not follow the same route as the prehistoric track, the Port Way, taking a line somewhat lower down the eastern ridge of the Arrow Valley. It avoided The Mount at Beoley — which therefore cannot be a Roman fort. It seems to have had the usual camps every twenty miles, or a day's march apart. Unfortunately the Redditch area is mid-way between Metchley and the small settlement at Alcester. No Roman settled here.

The road has retained its old name, or rather names. In the area immediately around Redditch, it is called Icknield Street or Ryknield Street. In Studley, it is called Haydon Way and, approaching the Cotswolds, it has the name Buckle Street. None of these names is Roman; if this relatively unimportant road had a Roman name, we do not know what it was. Icknield Street was borrowed from the more famous Icknield Way and does not appear in documentary form until 1275. Ryknield is a corruption of the Middle English *at there Icknielde strete*.

To the north of Redditch, Icknield Street is a narrow country road. Within the town itself, it has become one of the major roads skirting the New Town area of Winyates and Matchborough. Before the Development Corporation changed the face of Redditch, Icknield Street between Beoley and Studley had several of the features of a typical Roman road: it was narrow, straight, and ditched on both sides. Just after the crossroads at Ipsley, the road veered away from its straight course towards the River Arrow. This diversion may well have been a 16th or 17th century move so that the road served the Old Forge, where iron was smelted. The old straight line of Icknield Street was preserved in the line of the hedge. In 1968, before the Development Corporation began the sewers, drains and roads of Matchborough West, an emergency dig by local archaeologists found the Roman road

21

beneath the hedge. It was about 18 inches below the surface, cobbled, about thirty feet wide and with drainage ditches on either side. It is a pity that it has now all disappeared under the unfortunately named Icknield Street Drive, near its junction with Green Sward Lane.

It is worth remembering that Icknield Street was in use as the usual route from Redditch to Birmingham until well into the nineteenth century. It may have been narrow and muddy, but it had one great advantage over the turnpike road of 1825 — it was free! Two thousand years of usage is no bad tribute to the Roman civil engineer of Icknield Street.

The Roman legions left Britain in AD 410. They had been here nearly four hundred years, about the same length of time as separates us from Shakespeare yet, apart from Icknield Street, they seem to have left no mark upon our area. The Arrow Valley remained a wet, densely wooded, almost wholly empty land. It is during the post-Roman period, sometimes called the Dark Ages, and in the age of the Anglo-Saxon invasions, conquest and settlement, that we have the first real evidence of occupation of the Valley and its surrounding area. Unfortunately the period from the departure of the Roman legions to the emergence of a recognisable Saxon Kingdom of Mercia is poorly documented. For about a hundred years or so after AD 410, Romano-British civilisation survived in crumbling towns and remote villas. The attacks of Angles, Saxons and Jutes from Northern Europe, together with raids by Picts from Scotland and Scotti from Ireland became ever more frequent. The revival of the Romano-British under Arthur provided a fifty year respite before the barbarians flooded in.

It looks as if the invaders into our area came up the Severn and Avon. They seem to have been Saxons, and originally to have been drawn from a tribe called the Hwicci. Little is known of these people, though they may have had a tribal capital at Deerhurst, south of Tewkesbury. They were either driven out of Worcestershire by later Saxon invaders, or assimilated by them, but there is one piece of evidence to show that they reached the Arrow Valley. When the foundations of the new telephone exchange on Icknield Street in Ipsley were being dug in 1968, an early Saxon throwing axe was discovered. This weapon, called a *sceax*, was a Saxon speciality: it may even be the origin of the name Saxon. Dating from the 6th century, it is the earliest Saxon object to be found in Worcestershire.

The Saxons settled in our area rather late, when other more favourable areas had been taken. We know this, not from documentary sources, but from a study of place names. Almost all the place-names of the Redditch area are derived from Anglo-Saxon or English. As a simple rule, if we can understand the meaning of a place name without translation, then it was given its name by people who spoke English and the name is a late one. If the name requires translation, then, in the Redditch area, it is a Saxon name given to the settlement before the Norman Conquest.

Two examples should make the distinction clear. Beoley has an Anglo-Saxon name. It is not immediately clear that the name means 'the clearing where there are bees'; -ley is a Saxon word which implies an enclosure, a farmstead or a clearing. It is the commonest suffix in local place names, and clearly suggests that the newly arrived settlers spent their early years felling trees and cultivating land surrounded by woodland. The name Redditch has an obvious meaning. It can be divided into two syllables. Though some have thought that the original meaning may have been 'the ditch where there are reeds', it seems much more likely to have been simply 'the red ditch'. The name does not appear in a document before the 13th century, when something akin to English was being spoken. The ditch was almost certainly the stream known as Batchley Brook or Pigeon Brook. It still runs orange red by Forge Mill. The redness may be due to rust from a deposit of iron ore, or more likely be the result of Redditch's ubiquitous red clay.

The majority of the place names of the Redditch area cannot be immediately understood. They are of Anglo Saxon origin and they date back to the period before the Norman Conquest. Most are first found written down in Domesday Book in 1086, though a few are found in earlier charters. It is impossible to ascertain when they were first used, though the 8th or 9th centuries may be about

22

right. What they do provide is an idea of the landscape of the Arrow Valley in the period before the Norman Conquest.

The *-ley* names are predominant: *Beoley* is the clearing where there are bees; *Bentley* is the clearing where there is coarse grass; *Bordesley* is either Brod's clearing, or possibly the Bordars' or, cottagers' clearing; *Bradley* is the broad clearing; *Studley* is the clearing where there are horses.

Two other *-ley* names do not appear in a document before the mid-15th century, but it is safe to assume that they were originally of Saxon origin: *Batchley* is a valley clearing, and *Bridley* (Moor) probably means the bird clearing.

One other *-ley* placename has been lost by recent changes in spelling. The name Headless Cross, which has led the more susceptible to imagine a place of execution, first appears in written form in 1275 as *Headley:* as late as the early nineteenth century it was written as Headley's Cross. It must have been the clearing of some Saxon chieftain whose name was Hedda.

Many of the other names in the Redditch locality also have an association with trees: *Bromsgrove* is Brema's grove or thicket. The name Birmingham has the same pre-fix, though it unlikely that it was founded by the same tribal leader. *Callow Hill* is the bare hill, *ie* one devoid of trees; *Hopwood* probably means the farm in the wood in the valley; *Lea End* originally perhaps *Ley End*, is either the end of the woodland or the end of the clearing; *Walkwood* is another personal name, the wood which belonged to Weorca; *Weatheroak* is a name which has been the subject of some dispute, but the oak belonging to Wedera seems as likely a derivation as any.

The village immediately to the south of Redditch, called *Astwood Bank*, neatly sums up the impression given by so many of these village names: here is the wood on the east, that is on the eastern edge of the parish of Feckenham.

Placename evidence in the locality of the Arrow Valley leads to inescapable conclusions. The Saxons were the first settlers here; they found the area heavily wooded; they made small clearings and began farming here. This impression is re-inforced by the many local names which end in *Green*. This suffix is English, not Saxon, and is used for later, post-Conquest, names. New settlements came into being between 1066 and the onset of the Black Death in 1348/9, because the population probably trebled in those years. The name *Green*, like *-ley*, is a word for a clearing. Since almost all of these settlements are to this day tiny, it is tempting to suggest that they were clearings of marginal land, always likely to be unsuccessful and to be deserted when times became hard. One of these settlements gives a clue as to how dense woodland could be cleared. *Barnt Green*, to the north of Redditch, means the clearing which was burnt. No doubt fire was used to make the first foray into the impenetrable forest.

There are other placenames in the Redditch area which do not contain the suggestion of trees. There is one Saxon name — *Tardebigge* for many years the mother parish of Redditch — the meaning of which is wholly unknown. But the picture of the Arrow Valley on the eve of the Norman Conquest is now clear. Within a densely wooded landscape, criss-crossed perhaps by ancient tracks, a Salt Way from Droitwich and a deteriorating Roman road, were a number of small settlements, where a few score peasants earned a precarious living.

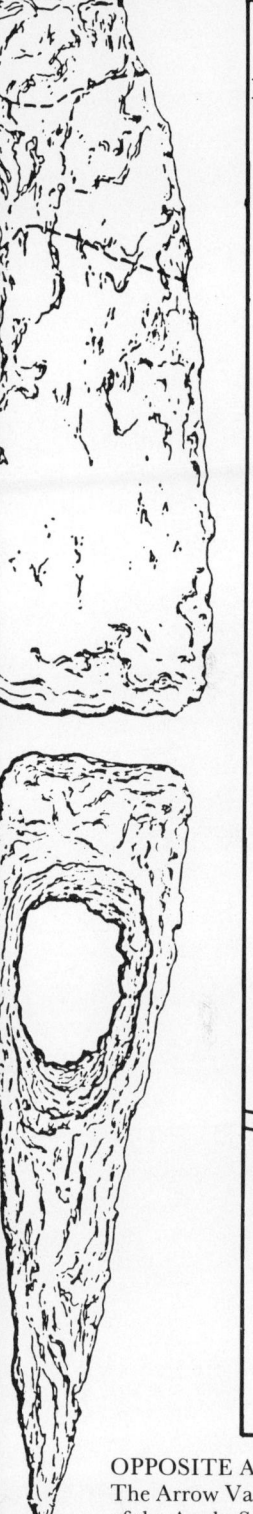

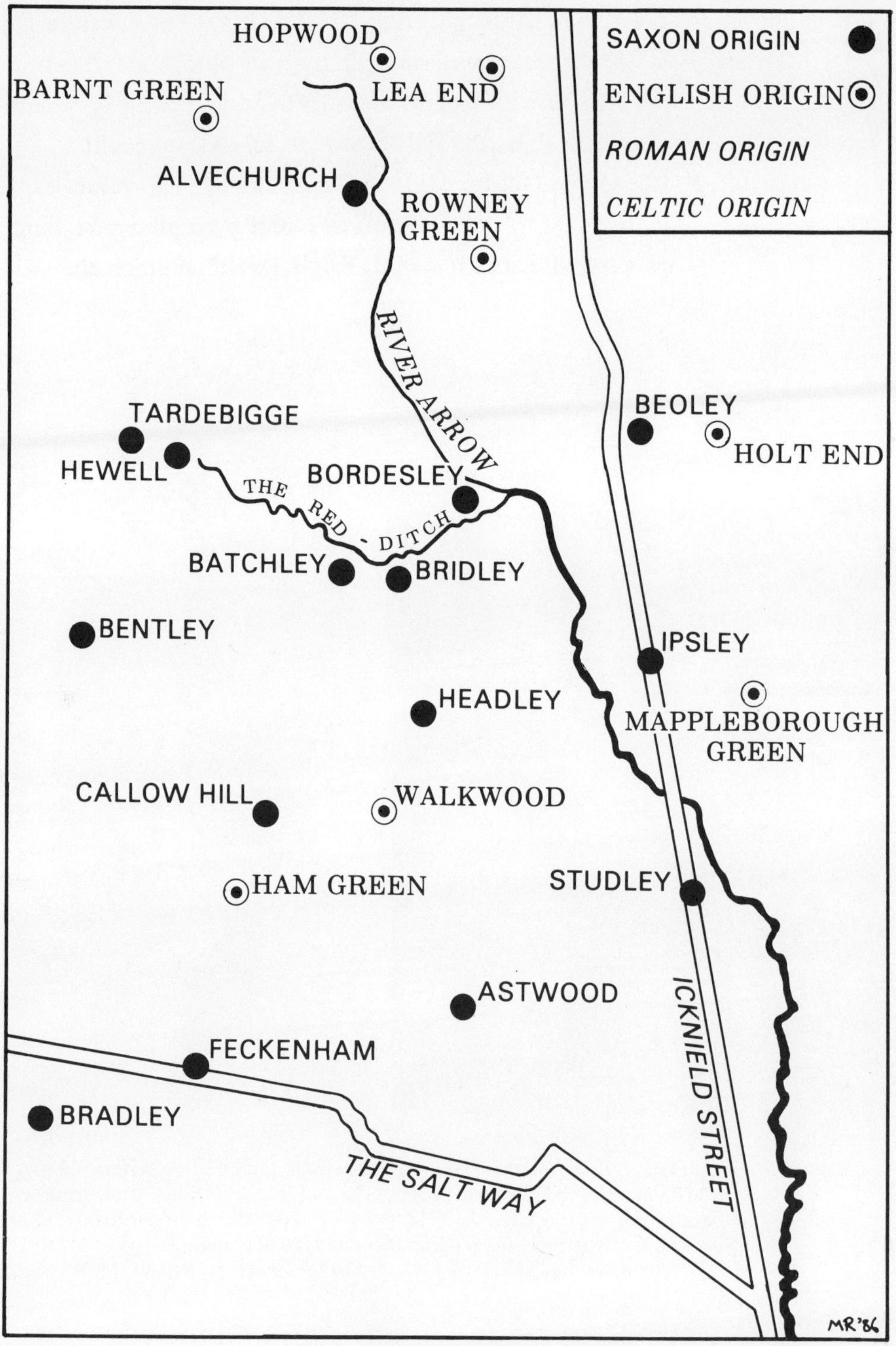

SAXON ORIGIN	●
ENGLISH ORIGIN	⊙
ROMAN ORIGIN	
CELTIC ORIGIN	

HOPWOOD

BARNT GREEN

LEA END

ALVECHURCH

ROWNEY GREEN

RIVER ARROW

BEOLEY

HOLT END

TARDEBIGGE

HEWELL

THE RED - DITCH

BORDESLEY

BATCHLEY

BRIDLEY

BENTLEY

IPSLEY

HEADLEY

MAPPLEBOROUGH GREEN

CALLOW HILL

WALKWOOD

HAM GREEN

STUDLEY

ASTWOOD

ICKNIELD STREET

FECKENHAM

BRADLEY

THE SALT WAY

MR '86

OPPOSITE ABOVE: The Roman cobbles of Icknield Street, revealed in an emergency dig in 1968. BELOW: The Arrow Valley — a wet, densely wooded, almost wholly empty land, once the Romans left. CENTRE: Head of the Anglo-Saxon throwing axe of the 6th century found at Ipsley. (Drawing by courtesy of Peter J. Fasham). RIGHT: The place names of the Redditch area.

Ｆ De.O. teñ idē Hugo. III. hid in *EPESLEI*. Tra. ē. VII. car.

In dñio. ē una. 7 II. ſerui. 7 VII. uilti cū pbro 7 XIII. bord

cū. IIII. car. Ibi moliñ de. XVI. den. Silua. I. leuu lḡ. 7 dim

leuu lat. Valuit. XXX. ſol. Modo. XL ſol. Algar tenuit.

Ｆ De.O. teñ Giſlebt. V. hid in *GRASTONE*. Tra. ē. V. car.

In dñio ſunt. ii. 7 IIII. ſerui. 7 VI. uilti 7 cū pbro 7 VI. bord

cū. V. car. Ibi. XXIIII. ac pti. Valuit. III. lib. m. IIII. lib.

ABOVE: The Domesday extract for Ipsley. (Reproduced by permission of the Public Record Office). CENTRE: The Old Rectory, Ipsley — a Regency facade on a mediaeval house. BELOW: Brick and timber barn of the Huband family, Ipsley, now in the water gardens at Matchborough. RIGHT: Tomb of Sir John and Lady Huband 1583, St Peter's, Ipsley, apparently destroyed in 1867.

Domesday

The first description of the small Saxon settlements of the Arrow Valley is found in Domesday Book. At Christmas in the year 1085, according to the *Anglo-Saxon Chronicle,* William the Norman, who had been King since the Battle of Hastings in 1066, 'was at Gloucester with his counsellors'. The *Chronicle* goes on to say that 'the King had deep speech with his counsellors . . . and sent men all over England to each shire . . . to find out what or how much each land holder held . . . in land and livestock, and what it was worth'.

Redditch itself does not appear in Domesday Book, because nobody lived here until some time in the 12th century. What we today call Redditch was a part of the manor of Tardebigge. Domesday Book tells us that Tardebigge had been part of the Royal estates of King Edward the Confessor before 1066. After Hastings, it became a part of the Crown Lands of William the Conqueror. Tardebigge was a large manor assessed at nine hides, (hide: a unit of valuation, equivalent to 120 acres), though it had few people living within its bounds. Only thirty men are mentioned which, with wives and children, gives a population of between 150 and 200. The most valuable parts of the manor were the seven salt pans and two salt boilers at Droitwich which brought King William a useful income. They produced twenty shillings annually in tax and one hundred measures of salt.

A more interesting picture of one of the settlements of the Arrow Valley is provided by the Domesday extract for Ipsley. Now a residential area on the east of Redditch New Town, Ipsley was a Saxon clearing. The most likely derivation is from a personal name — it is Ippe's clearing though the suggestion has also been made that it could be the clearing by the white poplars or, since the settlement is on an almost circular hill above the River Arrow, 'the upper clearing'.

In Domesday, the village was a manor called *Epeslei* and it is recorded in Warwickshire. Ipsley only became a part of Worcestershire in a local government reorganisation in 1931. It was a small part of a great estate belonging to a companion of William the Norman, called Osbern fitz Richard, or Osbern son of Richard, who fought with him at Hastings. Osbern held a vast number of manors and did not live at Ipsley. He granted the manor, in return presumably for military service, to one Hugh, who is elsewhere recorded as Hugh Hubald or Huband, and whose family was to live at Ipsley for seven hundred years.

There are four lines of Domesday devoted to Ipsley. These state that Hugh held land valued at three hides from his landlord, Osbern fitz Richard, who was one of King William's tenants in chief. It is doubtful if three hides means three hundred and sixty acres: it is much more likely that three hides was the value somewhat arbitrarily attached to the manor of Ipsley and on which Osbern's and Hugh's taxes were levied. A hide was probably as unreal a term in 1086 as rateable value is today.

There was enough land at Ipsley for seven ploughs, though only five ploughs are mentioned. A plough was clearly a valuable piece of equipment. Mention of ploughs in Domesday generally means plough teams — the number of oxen needed to work a plough and generally assumed to be eight. As large a number as this would be needed to make any impression on the heavy clay of Ipsley.

Hugh seems to have had a full plough team for his own farm or demesne and two slaves to work them, which was the usual number. Slaves may have been as many as ten per cent of the Domesday population. We do not know whether they were married, or could own any property; nor do we know if the Ipsley slaves lived in Hugh's hall or if they had separate accommodation.

There were two kinds of peasant at Ipsley — villeins and bordars. The former held land from Hugh in return for clearly defined labour services on his demesne. It is impossible to distinguish between a villein and a bordar, except that the latter appears to be lower in the social and legal scale. A bordar probably had a smaller share of arable land. The priest appears between the villeins and the bordars, and presumably laboured in the fields with the villeins. Though no church is mentioned, its existence is implied by the mention of him. There is no sign at St Peter's Church, Ipsley of Saxon work. The mill mentioned is not a valuable one, simply a water mill used for grinding corn.

The size of the woodland in Ipsley manor is considerable (one league long and half a league wide) though, in view of the heavily wooded nature of the Saxon countryside, hardly surprising. No doubt the measurements given are approximate, but a league was three miles and this area must have been essential for the supply of building materials, tools and fuel as well as for pannage for pigs.

Before the Conquest, Ipsley had belonged to Earl Algar, son of the great Mercian Earl Leofric and his more famous wife, Godiva. The increase in its value was from thirty shillings to forty and may have had something to do with Hugh's efficiency as lord of the manor — or be a reflection of 11th century inflation.

It is not too difficult to imagine what Ipsley looked like. It was just to the west of the old Roman road of Icknield Street. Few Saxon settlements were built astride Roman roads. A road, especially one with good foundations and a passable cobbled surface, could easily be the route by which enemies could arrive — far better, therefore, to build the village a little way off, and with an eye to the water supply. Almost certainly the church at Ipsley would have been where the present Church of St Peter's stands. The churchyard is roughly circular, which is often a sign of an ancient foundation. The Domesday church would have been of wood. Hugh's hall, also of timber, probably lay to the north of the church, as it still does. Ipsley Court has been rebuilt many times in the past nine hundred years. The present building, almost totally reconstructed by the Redditch Development Corporation in the early 1980s, had a wing dating back to the 16th century. The Hubands did not move their original manor house; they merely improved it. The lord's estate or demesne would be near the manor house. It cannot have been particularly large if it could be ploughed by one team and two slaves. All the villeins and bordars had to work on Hugh's demesne as a part of the rent they owed their lord. They worked for three days a week, though this often meant a half day rather than from dawn to dusk. At harvest time they had extra work, until Hugh's corn was safely gathered in.

When not working Hugh's land, the villeins and bordars attended to their own lands, growing sufficient for their needs, and a surplus for sale. It is likely that Ipsley used the open field system of farming, with each peasant having a collection of strips in the huge arable fields around the village.

Until the 1970s, when Ipsley was built over by the Development Corporation, it was possible to see the S-shaped ridges and furrows which almost certainly were the fossilised remains of these Saxon strips. When Ipsley declined as a settlement in the later Middle Ages, its arable was turned to waste or pasture and the shape of the strips survived. When mapped in the late 1960s, they suggested a three field system. It is tempting to suggest that Field Farm House, a seventeenth century half-timbered farm, now surrounded by Matchborough houses, was built in the middle of one of Ipsley's great unhedged fields.

As well as arable, the Saxon peasants needed pasture for their animals, meadow for their hay, woodland for their timber, and an allotment for their vegetables. Ipsley manor had a large area of woodland. The meadow was almost certainly the low-lying land close to the River Arrow. In the

1960s there was no sign of ridge and furrow in the riverside area, which has now been changed out of all recognition into the Arrow Valley Park. The outlying areas of the manor, between it and neighbouring Studley, Mappleborough and Beoley, probably provided the waste or common pasture for the grazing of cattle, sheep and goats.

The allotments or gardens were usually adjacent to the peasants' homes. Until the building of the GKN offices to the west of Ipsley Church in the 1970s, it was possible to see in the grass of a pasture field the faint outlines of the house platforms of the mediaeval peasants of Ipsley. Although the metalled road from the crossroads with Icknield Street went straight down the hill to Ipsley Mill, there is still a public footpath from the church, striking north west to the bridge over the Arrow. This footpath appears to be all that remains of the main street of Domesday Ipsley, passing between the dozen or so house platforms which was all that is left of the now-deserted village. The huts would have been made of wood and thatch. They probably lasted twenty years or so before renewal was necessary.

As well as Hugh's hall, there are other buildings in present day Ipsley which remind us of that long-vanished Domesday village. The site of the mill is still obvious. Two 16th century cottages are called Ipsley Mill Cottages: there are postcards of the early 20th century showing the water mill and its mill pond. The 6" Ordnance Survey map of 1884 shows a complex set of ponds beside the River Arrow: the mill leet still exists. The mill itself was demolished in the 1960s and, for a decade or so, the oak axle from the waterwheel was to be seen in the grass where the road made its sharp turn.

Domesday Ipsley's priest was probably a rector, and a house called the Old Rectory still survives in its own grounds on the eastern side of Icknield Street. This is an imposing Regency house, with the date 1812 on its water butts. The back of the Rectory is half-timbered and internal beams suggest a mediaeval foundation.

Finally, the great barn of the Hubands has somewhat miraculously survived. No doubt, Hugh's demesne produced a surplus of wheat, rye and barley. It was kept in his barns. One half-timbered barn was found in considerable disrepair by the ruined Ipsley Court. An imaginative planner from the Development Corporation decided to rebuild it as the centrepiece of the Matchborough Water Gardens. Despite the depredations of children, the barn, a typical Worcestershire example of half-timbering with brick in-fill, survives.

Domesday Ipsley grew in size in the Middle Ages. St Peter's Church clearly had aisles in the 13th century, built for many more people than the Domesday village. Decline set in, perhaps due to the Black Death or later visitations of the plague, perhaps due to the 16th century enthusiasm for converting arable to sheep runs, or it may be that a small settlement on heavy clay was never really viable. But for its Church — which lost its aisles in the late 18th century — and its Court with its apparently endless succession of Hubands, the village would have become one of Professor Beresford's lost villages. It did just survive — and today, thanks to the Redditch Development Corporation, the parish of Ipsley has a greater population than ever in its history. Enough survives, however, to remind us of Hugh, his slaves, his priest, and the twenty labouring peasants of the Domesday Book.

ABOVE: Ipsley Church and the old wing of Ipsley Court, 1906. BELOW: St Peter's Church, Ipsley: a mid-19th century water colour.

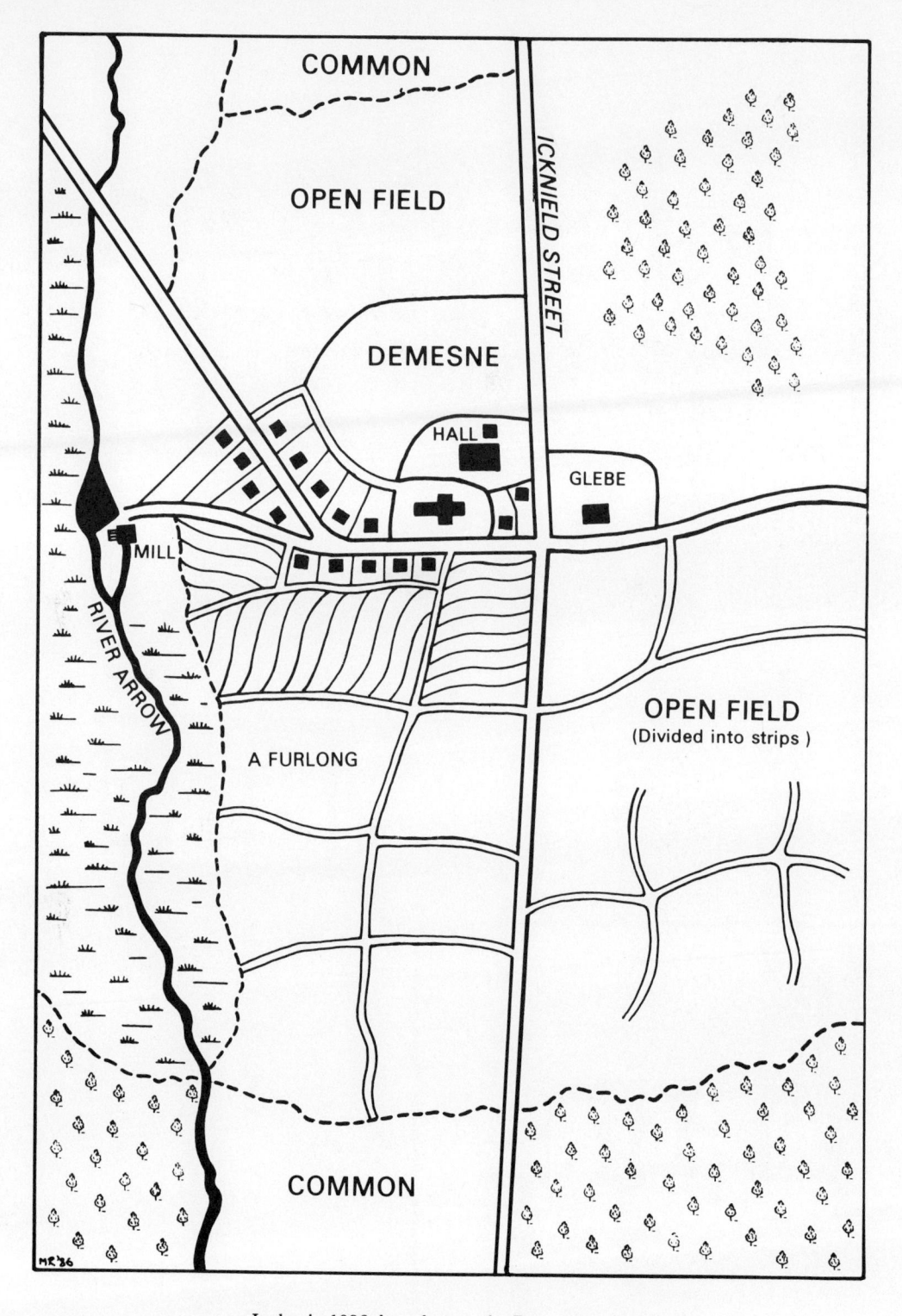

Ipsley in 1086, based upon the Domesday description.

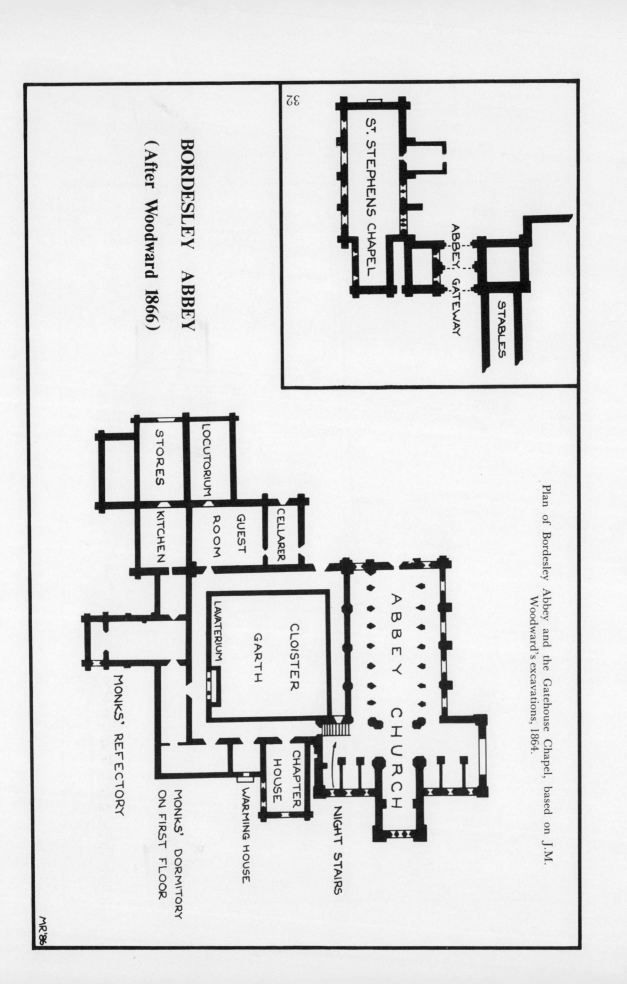

BORDESLEY ABBEY
(After Woodward 1866)

32

ST. STEPHENS CHAPEL

ABBEY GATEWAY

STABLES

Plan of Bordesley Abbey and the Gatehouse Chapel, based on J.M. Woodward's excavations, 1864.

STORES

LOCUTORIUM

KITCHEN

GUEST ROOM

CELLARER

LAVATERIUM

CLOISTER GARTH

ABBEY CHURCH

MONKS' REFECTORY

MONKS' DORMITORY ON FIRST FLOOR

WARMING HOUSE

CHAPTER HOUSE

NIGHT STAIRS

MR'86

Monks of Mettle

The first recorded people to live in the area eventually known as Redditch arrived on Tuesday, 22 November 1138. They were a group of white-robed monks, thirteen in all, and they came from Garendon Abbey in Leicestershire. They were given the Royal manor of Tardebigge. This included all the land now called Redditch and, in particular, an area called Bordesley. Whether anyone was living there when they arrived, history does not recall. They began to build wooden accommodation for themselves before starting work on an abbey to be dedicated to God and the Blessed Virgin Mary. For four hundred years, all but a matter of weeks, they were to be the most important influence upon the development of Redditch.

These thirteen monks belonged to a monastic order called the Cistercians, sometimes known as White Monks. In Burgundy in 1098 a group of Benedictine monks founded an abbey, in a remote and inhospitable locality, which they called Cîteaux. For some years they struggled to survive, but among their tiny number were two men of great ability. One was an Englishman, St Stephen Harding, Abbot of Cîteaux 1109-1134. It is almost certain that the parish church of Redditch is dedicated to this St Stephen and not to the first martyr of the Christian Church.

When Stephen Harding became Abbot of Cîteaux in 1109, an enormous expansion began. For the next forty years, something akin to a religious revival flourished, and Bordesley Abbey was a part of that process.

From Burgundy, groups of monks, always consisting of an abbot and twelve brethren, were sent out to found new colonies. Since several of the original Cistercians were English, it is not surprising that missions were sent to England. The earliest arrived in 1128 and settled in Waverley in Surrey. It was the relatively unknown Waverley Abbey which led indirectly to the establishment of monks at Bordesley. In this age of extraordinary missionary fervour, Waverley founded a daughter abbey at Garendon in Leicestershire in 1133. Garendon, in its turn, sent its thirteen monks to Bordesley in 1138. The process continued with Bordesley being responsible for founding the Warwickshire Abbeys of Merevale in 1148 and Stoneleigh in 1155, and Flaxley in Gloucestershire in 1151.

This rapid spread of an apparently austere monastic order is difficult to explain. Cistercian monks applied the Rule of St Benedict strictly to their daily lives. Their day was divided into three parts — dedicated to prayer and the Holy Offices, to spiritual reading and meditation and to manual work. They had one meal a day; they ate no meat; they practised, if not total silence, a routine with little conversation. Their buildings were of simple design, eschewing the carvings, the vestments and ostentation of Benedictine abbeys. They were linked by their constitution to the mother House at Cîteaux, to which every abbot had to travel for the Annual General Meeting of the Order. The Abbot of Bordesley had regularly to visit and inspect his daughter-houses, just as the Abbot of Garendon had to come at least once a year to Bordesley. Above all, the Cistercians sought seclusion. They played little or no part in local or national affairs. It is no coincidence today that the best preserved monastic ruins at Rievaulx, Fountains, Melrose and Tintern are all of Cistercian abbeys in remote areas safe from plunder.

33

It is hardly surprising, therefore, that Bordesley provided Garendon's monks with what they sought. The site was remote from any major settlement. If there was anyone living at Bordesley or Osmerley, settlements believed to have existed in 1138, but with no surviving record of population, they were speedily persuaded to move out. The site was in a valley, which Cistercians seemed to prefer. The River Arrow provided them with the prospect of water power; it could be used for sustaining fish ponds and, not least in importance, was its use for sluicing lavatories. The Cistercians gained a rapid reputation as water engineers. They proved outstanding in this capacity in the Arrow Valley.

Of course, the thirteen monks could not just move in and begin building. Bordesley belonged to the Royal manor of Tardebigge. In 1136, the manor actually belonged to the Empress Matilda, daughter of King Henry I, and wife of King Stephen. Matilda and Stephen were engaged in a serious civil war, but she found time in 1136 to seal a foundation charter for 'an abbey which is called Bordesley . . . in honour of the Most Blessed Virgin Mary, Queen of Heaven'. She founded the abbey 'for the love of God, for the souls of King Henry, my father, and of Queen Matilda, my mother, for the souls of my kindred and forefathers, and for my own safety'. One of the witnesses to the charter was Waleran de Beaumont, Count of Meulan and Worcester.

Waleran produced a second foundation charter two years later. Historians have been somewhat confused by two conflicting dates for the start of Bordesley Abbey. No doubt the confusion is due to the civil wars of the reign of Stephen. In 1136, Matilda was on the winning side; in 1138, she was not. In 1136 Waleran was on the Queen's side; in 1138 he was not. His change of side did not prevent him fulfilling what had clearly been Matilda's wish two years before. Matilda had provided the Abbey with lands at Bordesley, Teneshall, Tudeshall, Cobley and Holloway, the lordship of the manors of Bidford and Northay and the church of Tardebigge. Presumably, Waleran negotiated with Garendon Abbey and, on 22 November 1138, the monks arrived. No doubt, they prayed for the souls of their founders. No doubt, Matilda and Waleran de Beaumont, recorded as dying 'amidst the rejoicing of the angels', have received their just rewards. But they were not over-generous in their gift. If the land had been of any value, somebody would have settled there: they were giving away, for the good of their souls, a piece of valueless land.

Bordesley Abbey seems to have flourished. Within ten years the monastery was strong enough to spare at least thirteen monks to found Merevale in nearby Warwickshire. Its revenues in 1291 amounted to no more than £48 although, at the dissolution in 1538, Bordesley was the fifth wealthiest Cistercian abbey in England and Wales, with an annual income of £392. In 1332 there were 34 monks, one novice, seven lay brothers and 17 serving men. By 1381 the Black Death, almost certainly, and declining fervour, possibly, had resulted in a serious fall: there were only 14 monks and one lay brother. At the Dissolution, nineteen monks received pensions ranging from £4 to £6 from Henry VIII, with the Abbot, John Day, retiring to Beoley with £50.

Although nothing remains above ground at Bordesley, we are beginning to know much about the Abbey, partly because the site is now the most important ecclesiastical archaeological excavation in the country, the venue for a regular dig each summer, but also because Bordesley was the subject of an excavation last century. A Redditch needlemaker, with money to spare, who dreamed of finding treasure in the Abbey Meadows, commissioned the tutor of his sons to undertake an investigation of Bordesley with the intention, at least, of finding its foundation stone.

The tutor was James M. Woodward. The book he published in 1866 is an excellent example of what an intelligent, well-educated amateur could produce in the days before scientific archaeology. Woodward died in 1899 and is buried beneath the plainest of tombstones in Ipsley Churchyard. His name on the stone is barely decipherable; he deserves better.

Woodward realised that all Cistercian abbeys had the same ground plan. Before starting his excavations, he visited other monasteries, such as Rievaulx and Fountains: he read all he could about Cistercian organisation. In his introduction to the book, Mr R.S. Bartleet, the commissioner of Woodward's labours, described the start of the investigation:

'On a fine day in June 1863, accompanied by my wife and eldest children, the Vicar and Mr Woodward, and armed with a luncheon basket and the Rifle Corps' measuring cord, I proceeded to the Abbey meadows.

'There a pleasant afternoon was enjoyed in the fresh air and sunshine, time passing quickly, whilst marking out and measuring the ground plan'.

It is as easy today as it was a hundred and twenty years ago to see what Bartleet and Woodward were measuring. The Abbey Meadows, to the north of the town, have remained uncultivated grassland. The earthworks, remarkably clear on aerial photographs, are almost as clear at ground level. The flat rectangle, where Woodward began his measurements, and which he rightly said was the Cloister Garth, remains as clear to us as it was to him. To its north was the Abbey Church; to its south the monks' refectory. Woodward produced a detailed plan of the Abbey buildings. The modern excavations undertaken in recent years by Birmingham, York, Reading and Rochester USA Universities have confirmed the accuracy of Woodward's plan.

The plan, however, did not produce either a foundation stone or any treasure — and this was what Mr Bartleet hoped for. On 14 March 1864, therefore, Mr Woodward began to dig — or to be more accurate, Mr Woodward supervised the work of two Redditchians, who are not even accorded the compliment of a title or a Christian name in the book. They were 'Morton, a mason, and Twinning, a soldier who had been shot through the body at Alma' in the Crimean War. They made a series of exploratory digs, which confirmed Woodward's plan,   but they failed to find a foundation stone and they found no treasure. They did find a mediaeval tiled floor, which they removed: it was re-laid in the vestry of St Stephen's Parish Church where, somewhat uneven and worn, it remains. They found a most beautiful groined capital: this is now somewhat the worse for wear on Church Green. Most exciting of all, they unearthed a stone coffin with two skulls and other bones in it. Woodward assumed, without any evidence, that this was the coffin of Guy de Beauchamp, Earl of Warwick, who was buried at Bordesley. The evil reputation of Guy was such that he earned the nickname 'The Black Dog of Arden'. This discovery was the highlight of Woodward's excavation and led to a fine piece of purple prose in his book, which is well worth repeating.

Since it took some time to rescue the tiled pavement, the find had to be guarded at night. Even Woodward had to take his turn as night watchman:

'One night, it befel that no-one could conveniently take the second watch of the night from nine to midnight but myself.

'It was a dark cloudy night and the wind blew in gusts across the Abbey meadow, bending the tall poplars of the Forge to and fro, and then dying away mournfully among the pines on Beoley Hill. Though wrapped in many garments, it was too cold to remain on the mounds, so returning to the little chapel, and sitting down by the base of the square pier, I, like Sir Hudibras,

"Cheered up myself with ends of verse
And sayings of philosophers".

'This, however, failed at last to banish graver thoughts and the story of "The Black Dog of Arden", the grim Earl of Warwick, whose bones perchance they were that had been so lately disturbed, came again and again to the mind — his treachery, his vengeance, his murder and his burial at Bordesley Abbey. St Stephen's clock, striking the hour of midnight, intensified rather than disturbed the train of thought, when a louder blast of wind caused me to raise my head — and at that instant another head appeared above the heap of soil on the opposite side of the Chapel — it was the head of a large black dog. It looked at me for a moment and then disappeared. I seized a crowbar and climbed to the top of the mound, but my visitor was gone.

'Unwilling to add to the number of marvellous tales about the Abbey, I said nothing about my sable visitor. But he had already appeared to another, beside myself, in the dead waist and middle of the night to Twinning, who inquired the next morning if I had seen anything extraordinary in the night'.

It is a splendid story, well told, though sceptics may remark upon the difficulty of seeing black dogs, ghostly or otherwise, on dark, cloudy nights.

Woodward's excavations lasted a fortnight. At the end he produced an architect's drawing of Bordesley Abbey in the later Middle Ages. This is a skilful piece of work, reflecting his training as an artist. It is probably more accurate than the rather romanticised paintings published with his book. The modern excavations of the past fifteen years have not seriously altered Woodward's idea, though it now looks as if the original Abbey in Early English style was replaced by one in Decorated style in the fourteenth century. The Abbey Church was a large cruciform building with a central tower, originally rather low, but raised in the rebuilding. There were three side chapels in each transept. The chancel was long and narrow, having no aisles. The nave was aisled with arcades of pillars, in cross section, round or diamond shaped alternating. The night stairs leading from the South Transept to the Monks' Dormitory have been excavated and are in remarkably good condition for six steps. The external walls of the Abbey stand in places some ten feet high. The height of the earthworks at the west end suggests that walls of similar height will be found when the archaeologists begin work there. Present methods are much more painstaking than Woodward's. There is almost certainly work at Bordesley to keep the archaeologists busy to the end of this century and beyond. It is to be hoped that it will be possible to open up the whole of the Abbey ruins to the public in good time. They would provide the New Town of Redditch with a focal point and a sense of continuity with its little known past.

Today, Bordesley Abbey is a ruin of recently rediscovered walls and floors and undisturbed earthworks. It takes imagination to realise that for four hundred years it was home for countless monks and their servants. Of most of these men, we know nothing. The names of the abbots have come down to us: they suggest that Bordesley attracted local men into the monastic life, for some bear for their surname the name of a local village. Presumably, once the Garendon monks had laid the foundations of Bordesley, the Cistercian reputation for holiness exerted its influence on the Arrow Valley and beyond, as it did elsewhere. Bordesley was the only Cistercian house in Worcestershire. The much richer abbeys at Evesham, Pershore, Worcester, Great Malvern and Little Malvern were all Benedictine. Not everyone who found the Cistercian way of life attractive became a monk. The White Monks made a virtue of manual labour, but they had lay brothers or *conversi* to do the most arduous work. Indeed it was common for a Cistercian abbey to have more lay brothers than monks. It was the lay brothers who ran the great farms which ultimately brought enormous wealth to the Cistercians. These farms, often a considerable distance from the abbey itself, were known as granges. In the north of England, the Cistercians realised very early that, if they introduced sheep on to their granges, there was a fortune to be made from exporting wool to the merchants of Flanders, and from supplying the newly established English cloth trade. The same idea appealed to the monks of Bordesley. Most of their granges were in the Cotswolds, where the finest English wool was produced. But they had one grange near at hand. Hewell Grange, near Tardebigge, was the home farm of Bordesley, producing not only wool but grain and other food for the growing community. The Cistercian Rule was that lay brothers, not monks, were responsible for running the granges. Lay brothers, however, took some of the vows of a monk: they did not marry, they accepted monastic discipline and they attended some of the abbey services. At Bordesley, too, they worked in the workshops to the east of the monastic buildings.

Perhaps all Cistercian abbeys had industrial areas. Bordesley is unique in that its workshops have not been built upon, nor the site ploughed over. The fields to the east of the Abbey have long fascinated those who find the Abbey Meadows a pleasant walk. They abound in massive artificial earthworks. They were first scientifically photographed by the pioneer of aerial photography for the archaeologist, Professor J.K. St Joseph. They have been the subject of continuous archaeological investigation for the past fifteen years. The site shows that the Cistercians were great civil engineers, capable of damming and diverting the River Arrow and the Batchley Brook to provide water power from a huge triangular mill pond. They used the water to drive water wheels which operated trip hammers for the forging of iron. Bordesley may have sold its wool: it did not oversee the making of cloth, as far as we know, but it did make objects of iron, and possibly of other metals too. A sword pommel was found some years ago, bearing the arms of the Clare family, enough to suggest that the monks and their lay brothers made or repaired weapons — or perhaps they beat swords into pruning hooks, as Scripture exhorted them. It seems likely, too, that floor tiles were made on the Bordesley industrial site, for the Abbey church floor was paved with encaustic tiles, many of which bore heraldic or flowered patterns. If Great Malvern Abbey was justifiably famous for its encaustic tiles, it would seem that Bordesley was not far behind. There is no evidence, however, to support the view that Bordesley Abbey made needles. The theory was first advanced in the mid-nineteenth century and has been enthusiastically supported right up to the present day. No doubt the monks needed needles in order to produce their vestments and altar frontals, but it seems likely that they bought imported needles, like everyone else in the Middle Ages. No single piece of documentary or archaeological evidence has so far been produced to show that the monks of Bordesley made needles.

It is not too difficult for us, brought up in an industrial society, to reconstruct the daily work of the Bordesley Abbey workshops. If the power source was somewhat limited, the noise and smells and heat of the forges and other work places cannot have been very different from small workshops of today or the recent past. It is still possible today to see and hear a waterwheel operating machinery, within a stone's throw of the Abbey Meadows. It is, however, much harder to recreate the religious daily life of a Cistercian monk. Ours is a secular age: few of us have spent any time in an operational monastery; few of us attend church weekly, never mind daily, or seven times a day. It is difficult, almost to the point of impossibility, for us to put ourselves into the shoes of a Bordesley monk and to follow him in his daily routine.

The monastic day began with him in bed in the dormitory at first floor level. A Cistercian dormitory was plain — and, in these Northern climes far from sunny Burgundy, it was cold. The monk was woken at 2.30 am in winter, and even earlier in summer. From the dormitory, a procession of candle-holding monks moved down the night stairs into the church. About half the flight of stairs has been revealed in recent excavations at Bordesley. There is a full staircase still used at Hexham Abbey in Northumberland. The Bordesley monks walked across the tiled floor of the south transept, turned right under the crossing, through the chancel arch, and stood in their choir stalls and began the singing of the Offices of the day, the routine of services which occupied so large a part of every day and every week, month and year of the monastic life. Two services, Nocturns and Matins, preceded the dawn: in winter time, the monks continued, after a spell of reading by candlelight, with the first service of the daylight hours, called Prime. In summer time, there was time for a sleep and a wash before Prime. The most important service, Sung Mass, followed before the monks processed back through the south transept, through the door beneath the landing of the night stairs and into the large room, immediately below the dormitory, known as the Chapter House. Here they listened to a reading from the Rule of St Benedict, the textbook of monastic perfection. The Abbot, or the Prior, gave out jobs for the day; confessions of sins committed and good works left undone were heard and penance exacted before the monks left for their daily tasks.

Work, of some kind or other, occupied the period from about eight o'clock to midday. We may imagine the monks of Bordesley supervising farm work within the Abbey grounds, attending to production in the water-powered workshops, constructing the boundary bank which is still to be seen, diverting the river Arrow, or ensuring that building proceeded apace. In the first century of Bordesley's existence all went well. The colossal boundary bank was completed. The river was canalised, straightened and diverted to the north of the Abbey site. Substantial fish ponds were dug out, filled with river water and stocked with fish. Civil engineering schemes nearer the source of the Arrow were completed. The huge mill pond associated with the industrial site was constructed. Above all, the Abbey church and all the associated buildings of a monastery were completed. Somebody supervised the quarrying of stone from Tardebigge and Inkberrow: others ensured that fine building stone from the distant Cotswolds reached Bordesley. There must have been much work for the stone masons. A number of Bordesley monks merit the title of architect.

It was not until midday that a Cistercian monk had a meal: in wintertime, he had to wait until 2.00 pm. According to the strict interpretation of the Cistercian rule, no meat was eaten at any meal, but this seems to have been relaxed for the Abbot and his guests, and in the later Middle Ages it does not seem to have been enforced. Fish was eaten, and the Bordesley Abbey site to this day reveals a series of fish ponds which the monks constructed to ensure a continuous supply. Two of the larger pools were excavated by the Redditch District Council in the 1960s and re-stocked. A rectangular dry fish pond can be seen immediately to the east of the Abbey. This midday meal was taken in silence, except that one monk, who had eaten earlier, read aloud from some improving book. Each monk was expected to attend to the needs of his neighbour. The meals were taken in the refectory, on the south side of the cloisters. Before entering, the monk washed his hands at the *lavaterium* . Water flowed along a trough built into the wall of the cloister: it was another tribute to the enterprise of the Cistercians that water could be diverted from the river to ensure that no monk ever ate with dirty hands. Another channel of flowing water passed under the end of the first floor dormitory, where the lavatories were found. Bordesley monks certainly enjoyed running water and flushing lavatories, centuries before they were common for the people of the town of Redditch.

After the services of Sext and None, the monks had a further period of work. Some spent their time in the cloisters reading, or writing, or illuminating manuscripts. Though the Cistercians never regarded this work with quite the same enthusiasm as did the Benedictine and Cluniac monks, they needed books for study, for meditation and for the Offices of the day. A monastery had to copy or to write its own library.

The last services of the day were Vespers and Compline. There might be time for recreation and another meal. Bordesley Abbey had a room set aside for conversation, close by the Chapter House. Next to it was the Warming Room, the only room, apart from the infirmary and the Guests' Rooms, where there was a fire. The monks retired to bed at about 6.30 pm in winter and two hours later in summer.

This was the routine followed every day at Bordesley Abbey from 22 November 1138 to 17 July 1538. Sundays and Feast Days were a little different, with less manual work: Lent and other Fast Days saw still greater austerity. There is no doubt that this apparently gruelling, stultifying daily regime appealed to many in the first century after the founding of Bordesley. The community may well have numbered about 100. As is usual with religious communities, the initial enthusiasm did not last. No doubt the wealth provided by the Cotswold sheep proved a sore temptation. It was easy to overload the lay brethren and to seek an easier life. The Black Death of 1348/9 had a devastating effect upon England and upon monasteries, in particular. Perhaps one third of the population succumbed to the bubonic plague; its ravages were still more severe in closed communities. In 1381 Bordesley Abbey had only fourteen monks and one lay brother. It must have been difficult for so small a group to preserve the monastic routine. We know that, in one particular field, they failed.

The site selected for the Abbey must always have presented problems of flooding. Before 1350, Cistercian civil engineering provided first class drainage. After 1350 the dikes and drains were untended and the site became waterlogged. The recent archaeological investigations have shown that the Abbey church began to sink in the late fourteenth century. Instead of improving the drainage, the monks raised the floor level. They had to do this four times, and still they could not keep the church dry. Each floor level was cruder than the one below; on one, the archaeologists found a layer of accumulated dust and rubbish. By the mid-fifteenth century, it looks as if it was beyond the small community even to keep the church clean. That it was appallingly damp and unhealthy has been revealed in the skeletons of monks which have been found in the excavations. Pathologists have concluded that few monks reached old age and that all suffered from osteo-arthritis, rheumatism and appalling teeth.

Despite declining enthusiasm for the strict adherence to the Cistercian way of life, there is no evidence to suggest that Bordesley was a lax abbey. There had been two scandals in the fourteenth century. In 1312 one Alice de Estack complained of the grievous wrong she had suffered from a Bordesley monk, but history does not record what the monk had done. More seriously, in 1339, Henry Mason, a monk at Bordesley, received a Royal pardon for having caused the death of William de Warndone, another monk. That must surely have upset the calm of the cloisters, but for most of the four hundred years of Bordesley's existence we have little record and must presume that the daily round of prayer, meditation and labour continued.

We have one tantalising glimpse of an abbot of Bordesley. Most presumably died in office, were buried in the Abbey and their tombs were destroyed at the Dissolution. One was apparently buried in the Gatehouse Chapel of St Stephen, for his tomb was smashed in 1805 when the Gatehouse Chapel was razed to the ground. One, however, was buried at Hinton on the Green, south of Evesham. The Abbot of Gloucester had a country retreat at Hinton, a rest home for tired and elderly abbots. Thither went Abbot William Halford, either for a holiday or for retirement, and there he died 'happily' according to the inscription on his tombstone on 12 September 1490. He was buried somewhere in the church, beneath an incised slab. Though once common, especially in Midlands counties where imported brass was expensive, incised slabs are now uncommon, for they wear badly. There are two in Ipsley Church which are in a poor state. The slab to the Abbot, however, is relatively well preserved, for at some time in its history, it was removed from the church floor and used, upside down, on the church path. It was re-discovered early this century and attached to the chancel wall. The Abbot is portrayed on the slab standing beneath a low triple canopy and between the symbols of the four evangelists. He is wearing the habit and scapular of a Cistercian monk. His head shows his tonsure clearly. His hands are at prayer, but across his body, behind his hands, is the crosier, the symbol of his authority, as Abbot of Bordesley. His face bears a somewhat puzzled expression, as if death caught him unawares. Though not ranking highly as a work of art, Abbot Halford's is the first picture we have of one who lived in Redditch.

Abbot Halford was one of the last of his line. With the coming of the English Reformation in the 1530s, and Henry VIII's desperate need for money, the monasteries were seen as easy plunder. In 1536 Thomas Cromwell, acting as Vicar-General to the King, suppressed the smaller monasteries, claiming they were no longer fulfilling any purpose. His inspection of the larger monasteries found little fault at Bordesley. Indeed, in the Act of Parliament of 1536 dissolving the lesser monasteries, those like Bordesley were praised for their faithfulness. The praise availed them little. Bordesley Abbey had an income of £392 8s 6d and this appealed to the mercenary mind of Henry VIII. The larger monasteries were subjected to pressure from the somewhat repellent characters Cromwell employed to close down abbeys. A few abbots were hanged on their abbey steps, but martydom was not for John Day, the last Abbot of Bordesley. He announced his resignation 'for that he is aged, impotent, sick and also not of perfect remembrance'. This old man must have found Cromwell's thugs implacable. On Wednesday 17 July 1538 he surrendered his Abbey to the King and accepted a pension of £50. His nineteen brethren were dispersed, having pensions of between £4 and £6. John Day retired to Beoley, which may have been his birthplace. He took with him the processional cross of the abbey, a beautiful 16th century gold cross with Our Lord between Mary and John the Evangelist. This has survived: it was used at Beoley Mass House, a recusant's home, during the troubles of the 16th and 17th centuries: it eventually found its way to the Roman Catholic Church of Our Lady of Mount Carmel, built in Redditch in 1834. A copy is used as the processional cross at St Leonard's, Beoley. Abbot Day also rescued two of the priestly vestments from Bordesley, a pair of exquisitely embroidered chasubles, used in the celebration of the Mass. By a circuitous route, they have ended up at Downside Abbey, in Gloucestershire.

It was fortunate that Abbot Day did rescue these treasures, for little else survived his surrender. As soon as he and his brethren left the Abbey, the property and estates were forfeit to the King.

Unfortunately for Henry VIII, no adequate guard was placed on Bordesley Abbey and, within a fortnight, the people of the hamlet of Redditch, living beyond the Abbey gateway, had looted the building. A report from Thomas Cromwell's commissioners to the King described the Abbey as 'defaced and plucked down, and the substance sold to divers persons without profit to the King's Majesty'. The sale of items from the monastery did not take place until September 1538, by which time what was left from the Redditch scavengers made a mere seventy shillings!

A survivor of this orgy of destruction was the Gatehouse Chapel, dedicated to St Stephen. This had probably been used by those who lived near the Abbey as their place of worship. It was retained as such until 1805 when, in a ruinous state, it was demolished. There were probably people still living in Woodward's day who could remember what it looked like. He produced a painting of the chapel: it was a simple enough rectangular building in Decorated style. When Woodward's excavation of 1864 was complete, he commemorated it by planting a tree, a *Wellingtonia Gigantea*, on the site. The tree has flourished and is still there — just to the south of the new crematorium. It must be the tallest tree in Redditch.

Abbots of Bordesley Abbey

No complete list of the Abbots of Bordesley has been published. Only one has a tombstone which has survived — William Halford (1449-1490) at Hinton on the Green, near Evesham. The alleged tomb of an abbot in the Gatehouse Chapel was destroyed in 1805. It is not easy to distinguish between abbots with the same Christian name and no surname.

William I (from Garendon)	1138 - 1149	William de Berkhampstead	1317 -
Haymo	1149 - 1160	Thomas I (recorded as Abbot when Edward III	
William II (from Flaxley)	1160 - 1170	stayed at Bordesley)	1328
Haymo (returned from Redmire)	1170 - 1186	John de Peyto	1339
William II (returned from Kingswood)	1186 - 1188	Thomas II	1346
Richard I	1188 - 1196	Richard II	1349
William de Stanley	1196 - 1204	William de Edvaston	1350 - 1361
William de Pershore	1205 - 1212	John de Acton	1361 - 1367 (deposed)
William de Campden	1212 - 1217	John de Bradrugge	1364 - 1384
Philip I	1217 - 1223	Richard III	1384 - 1415
Philip II	1223 - 1244	John	1415 - 1433
Ralph de Buttesdon	1244	Richard de Feckenham	1433 - 1445
Philip III	1244 - 1265	John Wykin	1445 - 1449
Henry	1265 - 1277	William Halford	1449 - 1490
Thomas de Orlecote	1277 - 1293	Richard IV	1490 - 1511
William de Heyford	1293 - 1309	John Day (John of Beoley)	1511 - 1538
John de Edvaston	1309 - 1317		

The monks who received pensions from Henry VIII on the dissolution of Bordesley Abbey in 1538 were:

Abbot John Day

William Austin	Richard Bager
Thomas Baxter	William Edwards
Richard Evance	John Hantum
John Johnson	Thomas Lyllie
John Pene (or Gonne)	Thomas Philips
Roger Shakespear	Richard Soufford
William Steward	Thomas Taylor
Thomas Taylor	Thomas Wall
Richard Whittington (or Weston)	Thomas (or Richard) Yardley

Richard Whittington, the cellarer of Bordesley, is reported as Vicar of Beoley in 1539. A Thomas Yardley was Vicar of Tardebigge 1546-1558. Abbot John Day is reputed to have retired to Beoley under the protection of the Sheldon family. The fate of the rest is unknown.

ABOVE: Bordesley Abbey in the 14th century: frontispiece of J.M. Woodward's book, 1866. BELOW: Examples of encaustic tiles found by J.M. Woodward at Bordesley Abbey, 1864.

LEFT: The memorial to R.S. Bartleet, needlemaker, who financed the Woodward excavations of Bordesley Abbey in 1864. RIGHT: J.M. Woodward's illustration of a Cistercian lay brother, 1866. BELOW: Bordesley Abbey fishponds, re-excavated by Redditch Council in the 1960s.

ABOVE: The Gatehouse Chapel of St Stephen, Bordesley Abbey, from Nash's *Worcestershire* 1781-2. LEFT: Capital discovered in the Bordesley Abbey excavations by J.M. Woodward 1864, now by St Stephen's Church. RIGHT: The Beoley copy of the early 16th century processional cross from Bordesley Abbey.

LEFT: Cloister walls, Bordesley Abbey, revealed by recent excavations. RIGHT: Mediaeval stone coffin, Bordesley Abbey: almost certainly the coffin which occasioned the Black Dog of Arden ghost story. BELOW: J.M. Woodward's illustration of 1866.

ABOVE: Beoley, to which Abbot John Day fled in 1538. BELOW: J.M. Woodward's illustration of 'The Last Monk' at the dissolution of Bordesley Abbey.

Sheldon tapestry map border, showing the arms of the Sheldon family.
(Reproduced by courtesy of the Board of Trustees of the Victoria and Albert
Museum).

The Weaving Sheldons

The closure of Bordesley Abbey must have removed the *raison d'être* for the small community which had grown up somewhere to the west of the monastery.

Until the arrival in 1542 of the Windsor family as the new lords of the manor of Tardebigge, Redditch was subject only to the somewhat distant interest of the King and his Receivers of monastic lands. They found little of value in the plundered Abbey and were almost certainly more interested in the valuable sheep runs on the Cotswolds. There was a vacuum in Redditch, which was quickly filled by the Sheldons from nearby Beoley.

Ralph Sheldon is recorded as buying 'a littel bell' when the Bordesley Abbey sale was held in September 1538. He gave a home to the poor, confused old Abbot John Day, who retired to Beoley, perhaps because it was his birthplace, more likely because the Sheldons were the most influential local family.

The Sheldons were from Rowley in Staffordshire. They were associated with Beoley from the mid-15th to the 18th century. Confusingly, the male members of the family were either called William or Ralph. Most of those who have endeavoured to write a local history of Redditch have found it difficult to distinguish these various Sheldons. It was a Ralph Sheldon who is first associated with Beoley, in land coming to him through his wife, an heiress, called Joyce Ruding. It was their son William who purchased the Manor of Beoley from Richard Neville, Lord Latimer, who had acquired it from his wife, Elizabeth Beauchamp. William Sheldon was a Yorkist, who followed the ill-fated King Richard III to Bosworth Field in 1485 and thereby lost his lands. They were eventually restored, for his will in 1517 records the bequest of substantial estates, including Beoley to his brother, Ralph.

Beoley is on a hilltop some two miles north-west of Bordesley. Like so many of the Arrow Valley settlements it has a lonely church and rectory, and some evidence of a former manor house, while the village of Beoley, known as Holt End, is half a mile away. The Sheldons had a house at Beoley from the late 15th century. They treated Beoley as their home, to which they returned for burial for the next three hundred years, but they lived here irregularly. Ralph Sheldon I lived much of his life at Abberton, Worcs, and later Sheldons had a splendid house at Weston in Warwickshire. Thomas Habington described Beoley in 1643 with 'the Church mounted on a hill, in the midst of a large park replenished with deer, enriched and grand with timber and woods'. He does not describe the house, called Balford or Beoley Hall, and no description or illustration of it survives. It was burned down in a Civil War skirmish in December 1643.

Ralph Sheldon I married Philippa Heath of Ford Hall, Wooton Wawen in nearby Warwickshire, possibly in 1500. They had six sons and five daughters. Ralph died in 1546 and his wife two years later. He was buried at Beoley and his tomb has survived. It is in the Sheldon Chapel of Beoley Church and was erected as late as 1600 by his grandson, another Ralph. Judged by his will, Ralph Sheldon I was a rich and succesful man: he invested in coal mines at Coal Orton in Warwickshire; he also took over the outbuildings of Bordesley Abbey and used them for weaving. He was so well established at Bordesley that the Windsor family, who were granted the Abbey lands in 1542, retreated gracefully to take up residence at the grange at Hewell.

On Ralph's death in 1546, his estates were inherited by his eldest son, William. This William was born in 1500, and married, at a date which is unrecorded, Mary the daughter and co-heiress of William Willington, wool merchant of Barcheston, Warwickshire. This marriage, with the lands which Mary brought to William Sheldon, made the family's fortune. They became wealthy as producers of cloth, the Willingtons providing raw material in the form of Cotswold wool. William Sheldon foresaw the popularity of tapestries to embellish the walls of those building new manor houses in Tudor England. In 1554 or 1555, he sent his son, Ralph II, together with Richard Hyckes of Barcheston, to learn all they could of the continental art of tapestry making. They toured northern Europe and it is claimed that Hyckes was 'bound apprentice to a Dutch Arras weaver'. Their industrial espionage was remarkably successful and they returned to establish the first manufacture of tapestries in England. Most seem to have been made at Barcheston, which is near Shipston on Stour, by Richard Hyckes, who is described in William Sheldon's will in 1569/70 as 'the only author and beginner of this Art within the realm . . . a trade which will be greatly beneficial to this Commonwealth to train youth in'. Hyckes may have encouraged some Flemings to come to England to help launch the enterprise. Both Mary Tudor and Elizabeth I were keen to invite skilled immigrants to England. Hyckes lived at Barcheston until 1621, dying at the remarkable age of 97, having seen the rise and decline of English tapestry making. Whether tapestries were also made at Bordesley is not known, though likely. Bordesley had had its strong links with the Cotswold wool trade and looms were quickly set up by Sheldon in the empty Abbey outbuildings. Redditch could have provided the workforce. On his spectacular tomb in Beoley Church, the inscription records that he was 'so patriotic that he was the first in England to commence the Art of Tapestry Weaving for which at his own expense he provided large sums of money, and left by will property and money to care for the workmen in that craft'.

There are few Sheldon tapestries which have survived. The largest were wall hangings for the very wealthy. No doubt they faded, or fell out of fashion, and it is therefore not surprising that few people have seen one. A number are preserved in the Victoria and Albert Museum in London. Huge maps of English counties were the Sheldon speciality. The Elizabethan Age produced the first English maps by the cartographers John Speed, Christopher Saxton and John Norden. William Sheldon, his son Ralph II, or perhaps Hyckes, saw that they could be used as the basis for large tapestries. They produced one for Worcestershire and Warwickshire, which showed the Sheldon home at Beoley — somewhat more spectacularly than it really was. They also produced much smaller wall pictures, cushion covers, table runners and even glove cuffs, all in bright colours and usually showing allegorical or religious scenes.

Religion was to prove a problem for the Sheldons. Ralph Sheldon I had perhaps confessed his religious sympathies when he gave refuge to Abbot John Day, but his son William of tapestry fame, in his will of 1569/70, said he was a Protestant. He was the last of the line to be so, and it may not have been true. He had been MP for the County of Worcester between 1547 and 1567 and had seen violent swings of the religious pendulum; it may well have been prudent in 1570 to be a Protestant. His son, Ralph Sheldon II, born in 1537, after his return from his Continental spying trip, went to the Court of Mary Tudor, and shortly afterwards married Anne, fourth daughter of Sir Robert Throckmorton of nearby Coughton. The Throckmortons remained loyal to the old Catholic faith and, from the accession of Elizabeth I they, like the Sheldons, are regularly recorded as recusants. It seems certain that the Latin Mass was said at Beoley, at a Mass-House, if not in the Church itself, and Ralph found himself in increasing trouble as the reign of Elizabeth lengthened and the Spanish Catholic threat to her throne increased.

In 1580 he was put into Marshalsea Prison for recusancy and only released on the petition of his wife who, no doubt, had some influence, her brother Sir Nicholas Throckmorton having been

Queen Elizabeth's Ambassador to France and a firm Protestant. Ralph Sheldon was released into the custody of the Dean of Westminster, who persuaded him 'to repair unto the churche and in all things to serve and obey her Highness as becometh a dutifull subjecte'. The change of heart was not a lasting one. Ralph was reported again to the Privy Council in 1587, named in State Papers as a recusant, and was alleged to have been implicated in plots to overthrow Elizabeth in 1594. Cardinal Allen, leader of the exiled English Catholics on the Continent, is supposed to have described Ralph Sheldon as 'as good a Catholic as any in England'. If so, it could have sentenced him to death for, after the Spanish Armada, to be a Catholic was to be a traitor. Perhaps the enquiries of Queen Elizabeth's special branch persuaded Ralph Sheldon to be more circumspect, for he played no part in the Essex Rebellion of 1599, nor was he implicated in the Gunpowder Plot of 1605 which so closely involved the nearby Coughton Court of the Throckmortons.

Ralph Sheldon II may well have been too busy in the 1590s seeing to the construction of the family chapel at Beoley. The chapel, which is really a north aisle, was added to the Church some time before 1600. Ralph was determined that his notable family should be commemorated in a spectacular way. He erected black marble tombs to his grandfather and great-grandfather, filling the north arcade of the chancel with two superb Renaissance tombs. Nearest to the altar is the monument to his father and mother, with William Sheldon II being shown somewhat incongruously in plate armour, which he almost certainly never wore. The finest of the Sheldon tombs is that to Ralph himself and to his wife, Anne Throckmorton. Anne died before her husband, and he married a second time. Ralph and Anne had ten children — one son and nine daughters — which must have done much to reduce the Sheldon fortune by the provision of dowries. When Ralph died on 30 March 1613, at the age of 76, he had 136 descendants! In his will he 'protested to live and by Godes grace and assistance doe hope to die in the unitie of the Catholicke Churche' and he asked to be buried in the north aisle of the Church of Beoley lately 'erected and builded by me And in the Tombe laste erected wherein my wife lyethe'. It is a magnificent example of the workshops of Southwark, then just outside London.

Ralph's death seems to have marked the end of the great days of the Sheldon family. Few tapestries were made after 1614. His only son, Edward Sheldon I (1558-1643) spent much of his life abroad: he, too, was a Catholic but chose to be buried at Beoley. His eldest son, baptised William in the family tradition, was born in 1588/9 and lived through the English Civil War, dying in 1659. He was loyal to the Royalist Cause, and lost Beoley Hall in consequence. He wrote 'In December following [1643] my house at Beoley in Worcestershire was burnt to the ground and all my goods and cattle there plundered by the soldiers to a very great value, besides the incurable loss of my chiefest evidence and court rolls consumed by fire'. This incident seems to have been the only one involving the Redditch area in the fighting of the Civil War — and it brought to an end the active involvement of the Sheldons in local matters. Increasingly they lived away from Beoley, favouring their home at Weston in south Warwickshire. The family continued to regard Beoley as in some sense their ancestral home, insisting on being buried there. William Sheldon III died at Weston in 1659, but had an enormous two day funeral procession to Beoley. His son, Ralph III (1623-1684), was a great antiquarian, whose marriage in 1647 was celebrated by the weaving of a tapestry map of Oxfordshire and Berkshire, with the arms of Sheldon impaling those of Savage, in honour of his wife Henrietta Maria Savage. This Ralph Sheldon, known as 'The Great Sheldon', fought with Prince Charles at the Battle of Worcester in 1651 and may even have played some part in the escape by the Royal oak. But he spent most of his life at Weston, dying there on 24 June 1684. He too had a staggeringly expensive funeral procession to Beoley, where he is commemorated by a modest memorial with the inscription:

'Quondam Radulphus Sheldon,   (Once Ralph Sheldon,
'Nunc cinis, pulvis, nihil'   Now ashes, dust, nothing)

It seems a fitting epitaph to a family whose influence had been felt in the Redditch area for a century and a half.

LEFT: William Sheldon 1570, the founder of the tapestry-weaving enterprise: tomb in the Sheldon Chapel, Beoley. RIGHT: Ralph Sheldon (1623-1684), whose marriage was commemorated by the weaving of the last of the great tapestry maps. Painting in St. Leonard's, Beoley. BELOW: Sheldon Tapestry of fun and games on the village green. (By courtesy of the Trustees of the Victoria and Albert Museum).

50

At the Red-dyche

The building of an abbey tended to encourage laymen to settle near its gates. Despite their love of solitude, the Cistercians were unable, and perhaps unwilling to discourage people from moving near to their monasteries. An abbey, especially during its early years of construction, needed labourers. Though the Cistercians held physical work in high esteem, and invited lay brothers to share in their work and to take some of their vows, there must always have been a number of jobs for the mediaeval peasant to undertake. Bordesley had its massive civil engineering schemes, its industrial site, its fields, its sheep and cattle, possibly even some quarrying for iron ore, and it is hardly surprising that a small settlement grew up to the west of the Abbey site. It is first mentioned in 1200 by a monk who felt he had to give the hamlet the dignity of a latin name — he called it *Rubeo Fossato* . Fifty years later the name is recorded in the language of the native population as *La Red-dyche*. These settlers in their wattle and daub thatched huts would not have been tolerated within the grounds of the Abbey. So they lived on the banks of the Red Ditch. It is possible, even today, to find this feature. Batchley Brook or Pigeon's Brook still flows into the Abbey Meadows, and its waters, whether because of clay or the rust from iron deposits, still flow a somewhat alarming orange red.

Our knowledge of this small community is scanty. It survived throughout the monastic years, sharing the good times and the bad times of Bordesley. It saw the dissolution of the Abbey as a mixed blessing. The source of work, wealth, protection and social welfare disappeared overnight but many a hut, cottage and barn benefited from newly acquired stone foundations, tiled floors, roof timbers and glass windows.

Somehow the small settlement survived the shock of Dissolution. It witnessed the arrival of the new Lord of the Manor, Lord Windsor in 1542, and his precipitate departure to the greater comforts of Hewell Grange, three miles away. It has left few records behind. There is no indication of the size of 'the town of Redditch', for so it is called in 1625. The occupations of those who appear at Quarter Sessions suggest it was a small rural settlement. Labourers and yeomen predominate, but William Heming was an innkeeper in 1627, and John Woodyne kept an alehouse in 1628, when he was forbidden to 'allow unlawful plays or games to be used in his house' by magistrates who appear to be laying down the law with a puritan hand. There are mentions of a shoemaker, and in 1636, several tanners. One of them, John Reeve, appeared before the magistrates 'to answer for a bastard child born in Beoley'. He later confessed to getting Ann Palmer, singlewoman, with child. The magistrates were interested because bastard children often became the responsibility of the parish officers charged with poor relief. In 1637, the unhappy Alice Hickman, 'being big with child' was expelled from Beoley into Redditch so that the parish of Tardebigge should accept the care of her child. The Overseers responsible for Redditch tried in vain to push her back. It was a harsh world in the 17th century.

It was an unhealthy world too, for in 1625 Redditch was visited by the plague. The outbreak was a serious one, for the people of Redditch were unable to carry on their work, and twelve neighbouring parishes had to contribute to the relief of the victims. The records are too scanty to provide more than a hint of the crimes committed in seventeenth century Redditch. Ann Sharp pleaded guilty to stealing a blanket worth 6d in 1635. A little earlier Richard Barker of Tardebigge stole two ferrets from Thomas, Lord Windsor. In 1640 George Hardinge was prosecuted for sheep stealing. A picture emerges of a small agricultural community, with a few of the labourers branching out into rural industries.

They enjoyed three different lords of the manor between 1538 and 1542. The Abbot of Bordesley surrendered his rights and privileges in July 1538, and all the land of Redditch became the property of King Henry VIII. In 1542 he arranged an exchange of estates with the Windsor family. Henry had been entertained by Andrew, Lord Windsor, at Stanwell in Middlesex. As he had done previously with Hampton Court, Henry broke the tenth commandment, coveted his neighbour's house, confiscated it and sent Lord Windsor to Bordesley. The obedient but disillusioned baron brought his family to inspect their new home. One can imagine their delight on finding a soggy field, with a demolished Abbey, and a collection of peasant huts at its edge. They fled rapidly to Hewell Grange which, being higher up, was at least dry. They evicted the former cellarer of Bordesley, Thomas Evance, and began converting a monastic farm into a mansion. (The present Hewell Grange is a Victorian country house in the Jacobethan style, designed by Bodley and Garner, and built 1884-1891). The Windsors lived at Hewell for four hundred years. They prospered, and became Earls of Plymouth. They rebuilt the parish church of Tardebigge in 1777, employing Francis Hiorne of Warwick to build the incomparable spire, visible for so many miles around. This was also the parish church for the hamlet of Redditch, despite its distance. It had the unique distinction of being half in Worcestershire and half in Warwickshire — with its schizophrenic vicars subject to the Bishop of Worcester in one part of the church and the Bishop of Lichfield in the other.

The home of the Windsors is now a Home Office Remand Centre. The adventurous, who prowl around Tardebigge churchyard, may discover the sadly overgrown graves of this once influential family. They are best remembered in Redditch for the street names which bear their titles — Lady Harrietts' Lane, Windsor Road, Clive Road, Archer Road, and oddly named Other Road, which commemorates the strange Christian name of their eldest sons. Bromfield Road and Ludlow Road reveal the present home of the family which for so long controlled Redditch.

The hamlet of Redditch was a part of the parish of Tardebigge, and was to remain so until 1855. The parish church was an inconvenient distance from the settlement by the Red Ditch. Before the Dissolution, the peasants had worshipped in the Gatehouse Chapel at Bordesley. It was natural that they should continue to do so after 1538. The Chapel, dedicated to St Stephen, became known as Redditch Chapel, and served as church for those living nearby until 1805. We know what this chapel looked like. Dr Tredway Nash, in his classic history of Worcestershire, written in the late 18th century, included a drawing. There is an even earlier engraving among the Bodleian Library manuscripts at Oxford. And there is a painting, signed by C. Woodward, the cousin of the original archaeologist of Bordesley Abbey, dated c1866, but which may have been drawn from the memories of those who saw the building before it was demolished. St Stephen's Chapel was a rectangular Gothic building of the 14th century. It had four bays, each containing a window of the Decorated style. The East Window was a plain rectangular one beneath a Gothic moulding, and was clearly a crude, late insertion. The second bay from the West contained a Decorated doorway. Woodward in his painting includes a wooden porch. The Chapel was tiled, with ornamental ridge tiles. The Bodleian drawing does not show the western bell-cote which appears in the Woodward painting. J.M. Woodward in his book has the story of a Redditchian knocking the ball off the bell-cote through the chapel roof in 1805, when the chapel was demolished, and it would seem that the bell-cote was therefore a feature of the Chapel in the 18th century. It is from this same source that we know that at least one Abbot of Bordesley had his tomb in the Gatehouse Chapel.

Another person commemorated there was Nathaniel Mugg. He had a brass erected to his memory in 1712. The inscription, in florid lettering, records his generosity in restoring the Chapel in 1687. Living in Redditch and wishing to worship there, Nathaniel found the Gatehouse Chapel derelict, and being used as a barn. With the aid of Thomas, Earl of Plymouth, whose responsibility the Chapel presumably was, Nathaniel Mugg restored it for public worship. In 1688 the Dowager Countess of Plymouth provided a chalice and paten. On his death, Nathaniel Mugg chose to be buried in the chapel yard, even though he had moved away from Redditch to Kidderminster. His will of 7 August 1712 provided money 'for the maintenance and support of a sober and pious divine of the Church of England . . . as parson of the said Chappell' who was to read Divine Service twice every Sunday and to preach once.

Nathaniel Mugg's generosity and the quality of his restoration work ensured that the Chapel remained in use for a further century. By 1805, it was described as in 'a very decayed and ruinous state and condition . . . that it has become unsafe for a Congregation to attend Divine Worship therein'. The Act of Parliament which assented to its demolition and the construction of a replacement described how. 'the inhabitants of the hamlet of Redditch have of late years considerably increased', and stressed the convenience of a new church to be built nearer to where people lived. By the start of the 19th century, Redditch had moved from the low-lying valley of the Arrow, about half a mile to the south, and a hundred feet higher up, to a plateau, which clearly offered greater comfort and convenience. The Act of Parliament appointed a number of trustees, who included the Earl of Plymouth, William Pitt, Earl Amherst, not the Prime Minister, the Bishop of Worcester and a body of Redditch and Tardebigge worthies among whom were two descendants of Nathaniel Mugg, whose responsibility it was to build a new chapel on the piece of waste land 'known by the name of the Green'. They were empowered to borrow £3,000, to be raised by the mortgage or sale of pews. The Earl of Plymouth gave the land, a rough triangle at the junction of four roads. The Vicar of Tardebigge was to provide a perpetual curate, whose stipend was £30.

The new chapel, which seems to have had no dedication but always to have been called the Chapel on the Green, was consecrated on 21 April 1808 by the Bishop of Chester, his colleague of Worcester being ill. Engravings suggest it was a modest affair, built of brick with a fancy cupola. The trustees apparently used some of the Gatehouse Chapel stone in the new building — and they had the good sense to move Nathaniel Mugg's brass. It is now in Redditch Parish Church — the earliest record to a Redditchian and the last surviving monument from the Gatehouse Chapel of St Stephen.

The Chapel on the Green was soon too small. It was extended in 1816 and again in 1827. Despite appearances, it could hold 1,000 worshippers. The 1851 Church Census records that 1/5 of the population of Redditch attended service on Census Day. The Worcestershire antiquarian, John Noake, comments favourably upon the demeanour of these God-fearing Redditch folk. This was in large measure due to two remarkable clergymen: Rev John Clayton, Curate from 1820 to 1842, and Rev George F. Fessey, Curate from 1842, who became the first Vicar of Redditch and retired after 42 years' service in 1884.

Mr Fessey was Curate when the decision was made in 1851 to demolish the Chapel on the Green and replace it with a more ambitious Gothic church. Henry Woodyer of Guildford was selected as architect: the old Chapel was demolished in the summer of 1853 and the foundation stone of the new church laid by Lady Harriett Clive on October 31 1853. The consecration service was led by Henry, Bishop of Worcester on 19 July 1855. The Church was dedicated to St Stephen, thus reminding older inhabitants of the Gatehouse Chapel they may have remembered from their youth. It was a large building in a somewhat undistinguished neo-decorated style. It had cost £6,000, and it was clearly insufficient. Its interior looked like a barn; it had no chancel worthy of the name; it had no bells and no organ; it was poorly roofed and the building stone, quarried from Tardebigge, wore badly. Mr Fessey's retirement was marked by the provision of a chancel screen and window, but it remained for the wealthy Canon Horace Newton to remedy the deficiencies of the builders of 1855. Canon Newton seems an extraordinary choice to be Vicar of a small industrial town. He built himself a vast and luxurious vicarage amid parkland in Pitcher Oak Wood, almost as if to distance himself physically from his rude parishioners. The house, called Holmwood, was big enough to fulfil the needs of the Redditch Development Corporation from 1964 to 1985. But Canon Newton did not merely spend money upon his own comforts. It was due to him that St Stephen's Church was restored in 1893/4. His restoration sounds more like a rebuilding. The well known architect, Temple Moore, was commissioned to build a chancel, a clerestory, new floors and ceiling, additional windows, a choir vestry, new pulpit and a Bartleet memorial chapel. When he had finished, St Stephen's looked as it does today. Since Canon Newton's time, the stonework has been twice restored, and a major internal redecoration took place in 1955, the Centenary year. In the late 1970s, in order to cater for changing needs, the west end was converted into a suite of rooms and a meeting place, known as the Forum. The 1980s saw major roof work to combat dry rot. Some £100,000 is now needed to put St Stephen's in good order again — some twenty times the original cost of the Church in 1855. The Church of England is unlikely to find another Canon Newton: it is a pity the original architect selected such poor building stone.

St Stephen's remains the focal point of Redditch. The Green, on which the 1805 Chapel was built, has survived. It was greatly improved in the 1850s with an imaginative tree planting scheme, in which the people of Redditch were invited to plant a tree for £5. Their successors today should be grateful for the generosity of a century ago. Those trees are now splendidly mature. Church Green was surrounded by rather mean cottages in the 18th and early 19th centuries. There is in Redditch Library an extraordinary description of who lived where in Redditch in the year 1776. It was written, in execrable English, by one Joseph Monk, a needlemaker and Methodist local preacher. He has the Church Green surrounded by half-timbered and brick cottages, with only the Unicorn Inn, the Fox and Grapes in the Market Place and the Crown Inn at the apex of the Green as substantial buildings. One row of these cottages remains — on Church Green East. Substantial Georgian buildings replaced most of the small cottages in the early 19th century. The Red House and the building now occupied by the National Westminster Bank are reminders of that gracious age. The building of the Smallwood Hospital and the Redditch Institute led to further demolition. Today the Church Green, the original centre of Redditch as it grew in the 17th and 18th centuries, has become the area for banks and building society offices, and thus has retained an air of restrained calm adjacent to the bustling new town centre. Pedestrianisation and the completion of an internal ring road in 1984/5 have preserved an attractive oasis. Ill-sited 'bus stops and appalling traffic signs are examples of twentieth century philistinism at its worst.

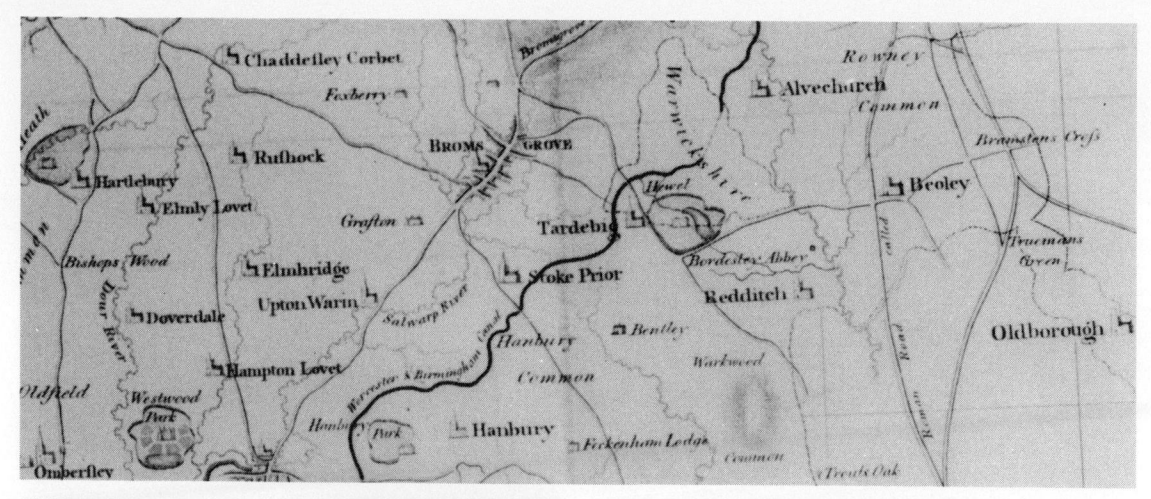

OPPOSITE: The Church Green and the Chapel on the Green before 1850.
ABOVE: Map of Redditch area from Nash's *Worcestershire* (1781-2) — one of
the earliest on which Redditch appears. LEFT: The mother-church of
Redditch, St Bartholomew's, Tardebigge, built (1777) by Francis Hiorn for
the Earls of Plymouth. RIGHT: Tomb of Henry, Lord Windsor 1605,
formerly in the Chancel of Tardebigge Old Church, and destroyed in the 18th
century . From Dugdale's *Warwickshire* (1661).

ABOVE: The family grave of the Earls of Plymouth, Tardebigge. CENTRE: Hewell Grange and Lake from Nash's *Worcestershire* (1781-2); BELOW: one of the last great country houses built in England. Designed by Bodley and Garner and built 1884-91, it was the home of the Plymouth family until after the Second World War.

LEFT: Monumental brass to Nathaniel Mugg, 1712, the restorer of St Stephen's Chapel, now in St Stephen's Church. RIGHT: The Unicorn Hotel, the most important inn in the town in the 18th and 19th centuries. (By courtesy of Mr J. Barker). BELOW: The Chapel on the Green from Prospect Hill, c1850.

ABOVE: The Chapel on the Green, 1808-1853. BELOW: St Stephen's
Church and Church Green, 1883.

LEFT: St Stephen's Parish Church before the First World War. Two Vicars of Redditch: RIGHT: Rev George F. Fessey (1842-1884), Vicar when St Stephen's Church was built and CENTRE: Canon Horace Newton (1892-1904), responsible for the restoration and extensions of 1893-4. From William Avery's *Scrapbook*, and annotated in his hand. BELOW: Church Green from Prospect Hill 1906.

LEFT: William Neasom, Vicar's Warden, St Stephen's Church. RIGHT: St Stephen's Church water butt, dated 1853, the year of major construction. The church was consecrated in 1855. BELOW: St Stephen's Church in the 1930s. The chancel screen was in memory of Rev George Frederick Fessey, Vicar for over 40 years. Redditch became a parish and St Stephen's was built during his long ministry.

To The Point

For the past one hundred and fifty years, the name of Redditch has been synonymous with needles. In the last century, the area between Alvechurch to the north and Alcester in the south was known as the Needle District. Though the making of needles no longer dominates Redditch manufacturing industry, some twenty million are still produced weekly, from four tons of steel wire. A surgeon may still telephone a firm of Redditch surgical needle makers with an order for a needle to fulfil a specific purpose — and have it made by hand and delivered for the end of the operation. There is a story — no doubt apocryphal — that when the Japanese began making needles, they named a suburb of Tokyo Redditch so that they might legitimately print 'Made in Redditch' on their needle packets, so great was the reputation of the town throughout Asia. It has also been said that Redditch needles helped to build the British Empire. In 1850 a packet of needles could be exchanged for a wife in the Sudan. Needles were easy to carry to the remoter parts of Empire — and the exchange rate appears favourable. When the Americans recently had difficulty in attaching the heat-proof tiles to their space shuttle, the problem was solved by sewing them on, using Redditch needles. The needle may well be the oldest tool known to man, or woman, but its applications are startlingly up to date.

There has been much controversy over the years as to how and where the art of needle making became established in the Redditch area. About a century ago, the idea was mooted that needle making was practised by the monks of Bordesley Abbey who, at the Dissolution, either settled with their skills in the local community, or taught the inhabitants of Redditch the complicated manufacture of needles. This theory still has its supporters, though corroborative evidence is entirely lacking. Legends of French monks touring Europe and the Middle East picking up tips about needle making are not historical facts. The apparently supporting link between Bordesley Abbey and Tintern Abbey, both Cistercian houses, in the latter of which wire drawing is known to have been carried out, collapses at once when the date of the first wire drawing is discovered to be 1568, thirty years after the monasteries were dissolved. There is no evidence to support the making of needles at Bordesley Abbey. There is no mention, in any records for Redditch or in the district roundabout, of any needle maker before the second quarter of the seventeenth century, four generations after Abbot John Day closed his monastery.

It is significant that one of the men granted special privileges at Tintern to produce iron wire was Christopher Schutz, a German, for skills in metallurgy in the middle ages and early modern period were found on the Continent. There is no evidence for the making of needles of any quality in England before the mid-16th century. All the superb English embroidery of the Middle Ages was produced with needles made abroad — in Spain, especially in Toledo, in Nurenburg and Aachen in the German states, and in Flanders. Needles were valued highly and they were expensive. One of the earliest comedies in English, *Gammer Gurton's Nedle*, shows a household being torn apart in order to find a lost needle. It was written in 1566, shortly after the first English needles were made.

It was Tudor policy to encourage skilled foreigners to settle in England. Both Mary Tudor and Elizabeth I were successful in persuading Flemings and Germans to bring their skills to England.

John Stowe's *Annales of England* of 1592 mentions a Spanish Moor, brought to Cheapside from Toledo, but he is a shadowy un-named figure, described as dying, with his needlemaking secrets unrevealed. Rather more substantial is Christopher Kinge, a Fleming, who established himself as a needle maker in London in 1559. He was prepared to teach his skills to others, and needlemaking flourished in the City. The London needle makers regulated their craft through a fellowship or gild, controlling its practitioners, ensuring the highest quality of workmanship and fixing prices and profits. The gild eventually became a Livery Company of the City of London, and received its charter in 1656, one of only two to have a Cromwellian rather than a Royal charter. The Worshipful Company of Needlemakers still flourishes and holds occasional meetings in Trinity Church, Redditch.

The Gild enforced its regulations long before 1656 and some members found them irksome. An unpopular rule banned the use of iron wire, insisting upon the more expensive steel wire. Steel needles were clearly better suited for their purpose but iron needles were cheaper and easy to sell. Needle masters who wanted to make the cheaper product had to leave London, for the Gild's ban extended over a ten mile radius from the City. Before long there were small centres of needle making in Dorchester, Chichester, Much Wenlock, Bridgnorth, Long Crendon in Buckinghamshire — and in Studley, a village some three miles south of Redditch.

It is probable that William Lee brought needle making to Studley. In 1629 a William Lee was indicted before the London Gild 'for the use of an unlawful engine'. Two years later a William Lea is found making needles in Studley. The spelling difference in the name is of little significance in an age when even Shakespeare could sign his name with different spellings. In the Studley parish records of the 17th century the spellings of Lee and Lea are interchangeable. It will never be possible to prove that the Londoner and the Studley needle maker are one and the same person. If only he had had a more distinctive name! William had a son Richard, described as an innkeeper and poacher, who had five apprentices learning the needlemaking trade — and every needle maker of the 17th century can be traced back to these apprentices. By the 1650s, men with sufficient property to leave wills are describing themselves as needlers.

Needlemaking in this area began in Studley — not in Redditch — but soon spread into the neighbouring parishes of Sambourne, Coughton and Alcester. William Lee, either by design or by chance, had chosen well in settling in Studley. The industry flourished to the extent that every other needlemaking centre in the country, London included, declined to nothing. The Redditch area ultimately gained its monopoly in the mid-19th century, when the final migration from Long Crendon took place.

It is difficult adequately to explain why this cottage industry should have succeeded so overwhelmingly. The Arrow Valley did provide the bunter pebbles which, ground down, were ideal for needle scouring. Studley was relatively near to the Black Country, the source of iron, and later steel, wire. The still flourishing local woodland could provide unlimited fuel in the form of charcoal. By 1630 it is likely that the Forge Mill, on the edge of the Abbey Meadows, and the Old Forge, half way between Redditch and Studley, were producing iron for anvils, hammers, files and other tools. The Old Forge, making iron with charcoal, probably by the old fashioned bloomery process, was sufficiently important for the Icknield Street to be diverted from its straight course south of Ipsley to serve the needs of the iron master. Though this forge ceased production in about 1730, it was still possible in the 1960s to trace the earthworks of its mill ponds and to find lumps of charcoal-fired iron slag. There was also a local market for needles: the glovers of Worcester, the cappers of Bewdley and the saddlers of Walsall all required needles, and the more locally they were produced the cheaper they were. Finally, of course, the Studley needle makers were free of the restrictive practices of the London Livery Company, and could employ any number of apprentices and journeymen, or use iron wire, or even 'use unlawful engines'. Yet somehow this does not add up to a wholly convincing explanation for William Lee to have decided — rightly as it turned out — that the Arrow Valley was the ideal place for a new industry.

Lee must have realised soon that the area could provide a labour force eager to supplement its meagre earnings from agriculture. There was much rural poverty and some over-population in the Arrow Valley of the 17th century. It had not always been so, even if Redditch clay 'was not, and is not suited to arable cultivation'. During the 16th century, it looks as if the Redditch area enjoyed agricultural prosperity. There were large stretches of commons and wastes, and no one appeared to object if squatters moved in, built a cottage and assarted some land from the wilderness. If arable farming did not pay, there was clearly great demand in the Tudor period for wool, and also presumably for hides and for meat, to feed the population which was, at last, rising again. A national population of little more than 2 million in 1500 had doubled a century later. There is considerable evidence around and about Redditch of yeoman farmers doing well for themselves, and building substantial farmsteads, many of which have survived to the present day. The great rebuilding of the century from 1540 to 1640 is represented in our area by Gorcott Hall, a beautiful mid-16th century house, of mellow red brick and with all the latest evidence of affluence in its fireplaces, chimneys and mullioned windows. There are three 16th century half-timbered farmhouses down Tippings Hill, between Hunt End and Callow Hill. 'The White House' is a typical Midland black and white house, where farming has been carried on for 400 years. Less immediately obvious as a half-timbered house is Lanehouse Farm, a quarter of a mile away, for its original front has been obscured by some 17th century brickwork. The deeds of the house go back to 1556, and the back of the house confirms its age. A further quarter of a mile nearer Hunt End is the pretty, black and white Loveline Farm.

In Hunt End itself there is a mysterious building in the fields of Lower Hunt End Farm, set within an area marked as *moat* on the Ordnance Survey map. At first sight a barn, the building has old brickwork with stone quoins, and looks much more like a chapel. This is confirmed by the other name of the farm, Chapel House. On the Blagrave map of Feckenham, drawn in 1591, the chapel is seen as part of a substantial Elizabethan mansion occupying the moated site, parts of which still survive. Here then was the fourth large house in little over a mile, which suggests rural prosperity in the Redditch area, though who built it and when it vanished remains a mystery.

In Tardebigge parish may be found a most beautiful and substantial timber-framed house called Cattespoole. It has preserved its original natural colours, never having received the Victorian treatment of black and white which we regard as typically Elizabethan. The house is almost certainly early 17th century. At Bradley, just beyond Feckenham, are three superb farmhouses, again about a quarter of a mile apart as at Tippings Hill. Each is a spectacular example of a yeoman farmer doing well between 1540 and 1640: the owner of Middle Bean Hall celebrated his prosperity by adding attic gables and a porch to the original house, and the date 1635 for future historians. Astwood Bank has another of these substantial houses, called Tookey's Farm. There is another at Weatheroak Hill.

All these houses, which so strongly suggest 16th century prosperity, are out in the countryside. None is found in a village — though there are some half-timbered houses of note in Feckenham village — and none is found in the built-up area of Redditch. It rather looks as if a yeoman farmer could make his fortune provide he could carve out of commons or wastes a sizeable estate. Of course, these houses represent the successes of this assarting initiative. We do not know how many came, tried to establish themselves and failed, but by the mid-17th century, and perhaps earlier, it is clear that too many had come to live in the area. The result was serious rural poverty. In the 1660s, 40% of the people of Feckenham were too poor to pay Hearth Tax. The population had risen by 160 in the century after 1560, a rise of over 25%. These people needed feeding. They needed a supplementary income — and part time needlemaking provided it.

The industry took root in Studley, Sambourne and Coughton. It was a cottage industry, with all the numerous processes carried out by men, women and children. There were many needle makers' cottages still standing at the start of this century. They were recognisable by their 'windows very wide in proportion to their height', so necessary to provide the light for the fiddly processes. Few remain today, though there is a row of needlers' cottages at Coughton, and a half-timbered row at Feckenham. Those that existed in Redditch have long since gone.

Almost all the processes in the hand making of needles could be practised in the home. Men, women or children, working with simple tools, were capable of cutting the wire, straightening the 'stiffs', filing a point on both ends, marking and eyeing the needles, filing away the burrs of metal around the eyes, breaking the needles in two, and even of hardening and tempering them. There may have been the occasional needle maker working in Redditch itself — for Redditch must have been at least as impoverished as the Warwickshire parishes — but there is no documentary evidence before the early 18th century. Freed of the restrictions of the London Livery Company, local needle makers began to flood the market with cheap needles, and 'needles deceiptfully made of iron wyre' so that the needlers of London were 'impoverished and like to be undone'. When presented with these complaints from the Needlemakers' Company in 1669, the government put a ban on cheap imports from Europe, but not from Warwickshire. So much did the men of Studley have the field to themselves, that by 1750 needlemaking was dead in London. In contrast, a quarter of the population of Sambourne and Coughton was employed in needle making, and a sixth of that of Studley.

Domestic demand continued to grow as the population increased. It soon became obvious that two of the processes in the cottage industry produced a serious bottleneck in production. Both pointing and scouring required speeding up. Experiments were made using horse 'gins: a more revolutionary idea was to harness wind power. The Sheward Brothers, the first named needle makers in Redditch itself, built a windmill on Mount Pleasant and harnessed it to their machines. It did not work, but the distinctive building known as The Round House survived for a hundred and fifty years. Much more significant than horses or wind was water power. And so the industry moved to the parishes of Feckenham and Tardebigge, to use the many streams.

There had been water mills along the Arrow since Domesday. From 1730 many of the corn mills were converted to needle making. Probably the first was the Forge Mill, beside the Abbey Meadows in Redditch itself. There may well have been a mill here in monastic times. Its name suggests it was originally used for iron making. The present building was built in the early 18th century and is known to have been used for needle scouring as early as 1730. It has a large mill pond, taking its water from the original Red Ditch. The power for the mill comes from an overshot bucket wheel. The present wheel, developing 104 horse power, was built by Edward White, engineer of Redditch. It was restored in 1983 and is remarkably efficient and quiet. The mill was extended in 1828, which presumably required the new wheel, which dates from 1830. Three main processes in needle making were carried on there. The most spectacular, requiring the considerable power of Edward White's wheel, was scouring. After the needles had been pointed, eyed, hardened and tempered, they were both rough and dirty. Several thousand needles were laid out on 'purses' of hurden or coarse cloth. A grinding paste of crushed emery pebbles, soft soap and water was poured on, and the needles rolled up into a sausage shaped roll, tightly tied with string. Two such rolls were placed on a flat table beneath a very heavy scouring bed. This was rolled to and fro by a rocker device known as a whee-whaw. The needles were scoured in the paste, which had to be regularly moistened. The process took several days, with the scouring paste changed as the needles became more polished. It is hardly surprising that this process was soon monopolised by water mills. Previously it had required men to scour needles by rolling planks of wood endlessly over the sausages — so lengthy a labour that they allegedly continued it while drinking in the alehouses. If no exact date can be given to the beginning of scouring at Forge Mill, a clear date may be given for its ending. On 2 May 1958, Albert Jakeman removed some packets of needles from the scouring beds, picked up his coat and locked the doors. The world's last surviving water-powered scouring mill had ended its economic life after two hundred and twenty eight years.

The other processes carried out at Forge Mill were barrelling and pointing. The former was merely the drying of needles, after having been scoured, in revolving barrels filled with bran or sawdust. Mr Jakeman left some of his last needles in his barrels in 1958, as the author painfully discovered in the 1960s, when he unwisely thrust his hand into a barrel of sawdust. The skill of the scourer was revealed, for his needles showed not a speck of rust, despite ten years' neglect in the damp mill. Pointing is the process in needle making which has attracted the greatest attention, for it was the most dangerous. In the cottage industry needles were pointed one by one, using a file. Water power meant that grind stones could be used. There is plenty of sandstone in the Redditch area. Stones were fitted tightly to a square axle; they were run off the waterwheel at speeds of allegedly 2,000 rpm. The pointer sat in front of the revolving stone with some fifty or more stiffs on his palm, covering all but the tips with his other hand. By rubbing his hands together he turned all the stiffs against the grind-stone, and they were soon pointed. It was very much quicker than the previous method — but much more dangerous. The grind stones had a tendency to fracture at the corners of the axle. If one did fracture, it took the head off the operative. In the north wall of the Forge Mill is a small stone incised E.M. 1816 — the tombstone of Edward Murry, who was so killed.

To watch a pointer at work was spectacular, since he worked in semi-gloom, illuminated by the sparks flying off his grind stone. But he was breathing in that lethal mixture of stone and steel dust. He wore a mask over his mouth and nose, but that did little to prevent the dust settling in his mouth, throat and lungs. The pointer earned high wages — between £2 and £6 a week in the early 19th century, when the average wage of an agricultural labourer was little more than 10 shillings — but he was not expected to live long. A survey by a Mr Osborne in 1838 showed that Redditch had 150 needle pointers, their average age was 28, and the average length of time at their dangerous employment was eight years. The motto of the pointer seems to have been 'a short life but a merry one'. Redditch needle pointers had a reputation for hard living and hard drinking.

'There draws the grinder his laborious breath,
There coughing at his deadly trade he bends,
Born to die young, he fears no man, nor death
Scorning the future, what he earns he spends.

'Yet Abraham and Elliot both in vain
Bid science on the cheek prolong the bloom:
He would not live! He seems in haste to gain
The undisturbed asylum of the tomb,
And old at two and thirty, meets his doom!'

Abraham and Elliot were but two inventors who designed fans and other devices to prevent what was know as 'Pointers' Rot'. The pointers would have none of the various fans, fearing a reduction in wages if their work was less dangerous. In 1846 they went on strike, against John Chambers' extractor fans: the strike lasted 12 months. During that year the needle masters installed the fans. Within a matter of months of the end of the strike, no pointer would work unless a fan was installed.

Forge Mill was, of course, not unique. Occupying an older building was Washford Mill, just to the north of Studley, which was converted to needle making at about the same time as Forge Mill. The pioneers were rapidly followed by Old Mill and New Mill, on the mill pond just to the north of the H.D.A. Forgings Works in Windsor Road, and Beoley Paper Mill, which made the special paper into which finished needles were placed for sale. Ipsley Mill, which had been mentioned in Domesday, was converted to needle making. In Studley, there was Priory Mill, and at Alcester both Oversley and Hoo Mills were converted. In Feckenham quite minor streams were dammed and regulated to drive three mills, one of which, Old Yarr Mill, became the headquarters of John English and Company, which virtually monopolised the needle trade to America in the 19th century. Between Feckenham and Alcester, a distance of barely ten miles with no river larger than the Arrow, there were at one time some 16 mills geared to needle production, an astonishing concentration.

Though none was large by modern industrial standards, these mills attracted workers. As the domestic and foreign demand for high quality needles increased, so the number of outworkers in the non-mechanised processes increased. There was therefore something of an influx of people seeking a place to live. By the late 18th century there was no more common land for the new arrivals in Studley or Sambourne. But there was plenty of common land in Tardebigge parish, in Feckenham and at Crabbs Cross, Headless Cross and Astwood Bank. The availability of building land and the concentration of work on the water mills led directly to the growth of Redditch. The hamlet became a township. A population of about 1,000 in 1800 had doubled twenty years later. When the Long Crendon needle makers, suffering too much from the competition, finally gave up and moved north west, they still found plenty of room in Astwood Bank and along the Ridgeway, both to build and to practise their skills. By 1850, when the Redditch area had a monopoly of English needle making, the town had a population of 4,518.

By then, of course, the limits of water power had been reached. It was remarkable that streams as insignificant as the Arrow could provide power for such a concentration of industry. By 1830 it was clear that there was no further room for expansion. In 1835 the first steam-powered mill was opened. The application of steam to needle making was extraordinarily late, for the Lancashire cotton industry was using Boulton and Watt engines sixty years earlier. The needle masters who adopted steam power built their mills, not in Sambourne or Studley, nor yet in the low lying Arrow Valley, but in the town of Redditch, where it was dry and where the workforce was to hand. They thus encouraged the movement of population into the urban area, and Redditch developed its 'dark satanic mills'. A few of these have survived. Argosy Works in Clive Road retains the grim air of a fortress, though it has lost its chimneys — and, of course, its needle makers.

The most impressive of these vast, steam-driven factories is British Mills, on Prospect Hill, built by Samuel Thomas in 1840. The facade has changed little, though today there is no sign of the huge chimneys which belched out smoke from the furnaces below. Unlike modern day industrialists, Samuel Thomas chose to live, if not over the shop, then in a substantial house attached to the works. Though today British Mills is occupied by a multiplicity of small manufacturers, it is not difficult to imagine its bustle, dust and dirt, its noise and its smells when it was the largest needle works in the world.

Almost as large was the factory of Henry Milward and Sons, established at Washford Mills on Ipsley Street. One of the confusing features of Redditch needle mills is that, when a manufacturer moved from his water mill on the Arrow to his new steam mill, he frequently took the name with him. So Richard Hemming left Forge Mill by the Abbey Meadows and built Forge Mills at the top of Prospect Hill. Henry Milward left Washford Mill, Studley and built Washford Mills, Redditch. Milward had been accustomed to transacting his business, and seeking skilled employees, at the Fountain Inn, on Breedon, now known as Ipsley Street. His new steam mill may have had the grand name of Washford Mills, but to many Redditchians then and now, the works were known as 'The Fountain'. Like so many 19th century mills, Washford had its clock tower and its bell, and woe betide any worker who failed to note the time or heed the bell. The Milwards were enthusiastic Anglicans, and Colonel Milward is still remembered in Redditch for stopping all work in the factory for ten minutes every morning for compulsory prayers. Notes were also kept of anyone failing to attend St Stephen's each Sunday. Henry Milward, however, was among the first employers in England to pay his workers on Friday, so that shopping might be done in daylight on Saturday. His trust in his workers to report for the half day on Saturday was not misplaced.

Steam power was uneconomic if harnessed to small factories. Large factories meant substantial investment, and it is hardly surprising that the move to Redditch led to the disappearance of the small needle maker, and his replacement by the capitalist entrepreneur. Even before the advent of steam power, the industry was dominated by six relatively large firms. Smaller firms only survived by making specialist needles or by concentrating on a particular process. During the so called Great Depression of 1873 to 1896, the number of needle firms fell from 129 to 111. It was still possible for a relatively small firm, A.G. Baylis and Co, to give its unsalubrious workshop a pretentious name like The Royal Needle Manufactory, Pool Meadow, Redditch. More impressive was its export trade to France, with a fluent writer of French for its letters to its Lyonnaise customers. Many amalgamations followed in the years to the First World War: brand names often survived — and indeed still survive, with their quaint 19th century trade marks and labelling — but the number of independent firms had fallen to 61 by 1913. Three of these were large producers — Milwards with 1,000 workers, Abel Morralls and William Woodfields with 500 each.

The process of amalgamation has continued to the present day. Even though the number of needles produced each week is about the same as it was a century ago, production is now almost entirely in the hands of Needle Industries — and they have retreated to the birth place of the industry. They make their twenty million needles, not in Redditch, but in Studley.

LEFT: Gorcott Hall, evidence of 16th century wealth in the area. RIGHT: The White House, a 16th century farm at Tippings Hill. BELOW: Lower Hunt End Farm. The Chapel is the last survival of the substantial Elizabethan mansion shown on the Blagrave map of Feckenham of 1591.

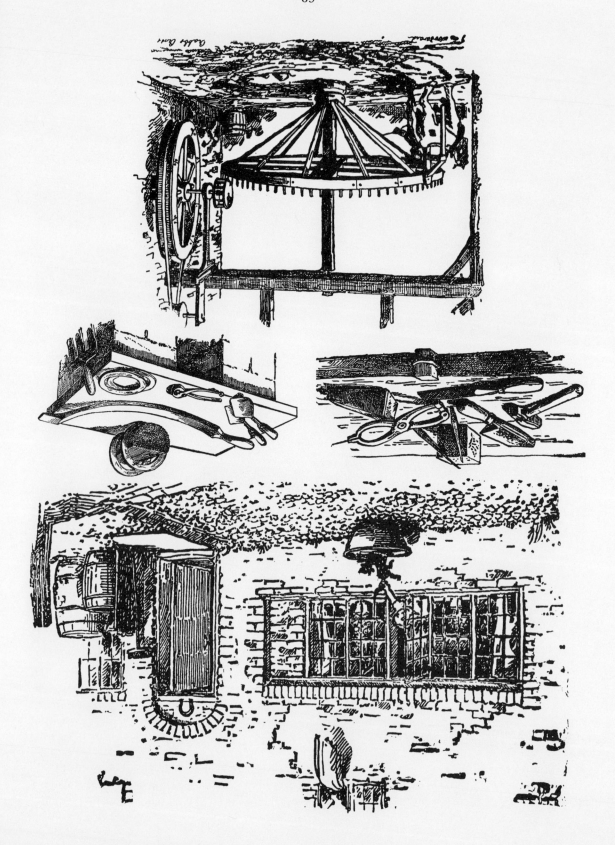

OPPOSITE ABOVE: Needlemaker's cottage, drawn by J.M. Woodward.
LEFT: Early hand tools for needlemaking. RIGHT: Hand tools for
straightening 'stiffs'. BELOW: Horse 'gin used for driving needle-making
machinery. Drawing by J.M. Woodward. ABOVE: Needlemaking: cutting
and straightening the 'stiffs'. BELOW: Needle stamping and eyeing.

LEFT: Needle pointing, with an extractor fan fitted. RIGHT: Needle hardening. BELOW: The Forge Mill — a needle scouring mill from 1730.

ABOVE: The Round House, Mount Pleasant, built by the Sheward brothers as an experimental wind-powered needle mill. BELOW: Paper Mill Walk. The mill pond is one of many along the River Arrow which used to drive needle mills.

ABOVE: Washford Needle Mill, Studley. BELOW: Washford Mills, Ipsley Street, the great needle works of the Milward family, known to many Redditchians as The Fountain.

LEFT: The home of Samuel Thomas, needlemaster, attached to his British Mills, 1840, the largest steam-powered needle mill in the town. RIGHT: Letter of 1841 from USA to John English and Co, Needle-makers of Feckenham, brought across the Atlantic in Brunel's steamship *Great Western*. BELOW: A.G. Baylis' Needle Works, known as the Royal Needle Manufactory c1890. Despite its humble appearance, the factory had a flourishing export trade to France in the 1860s.

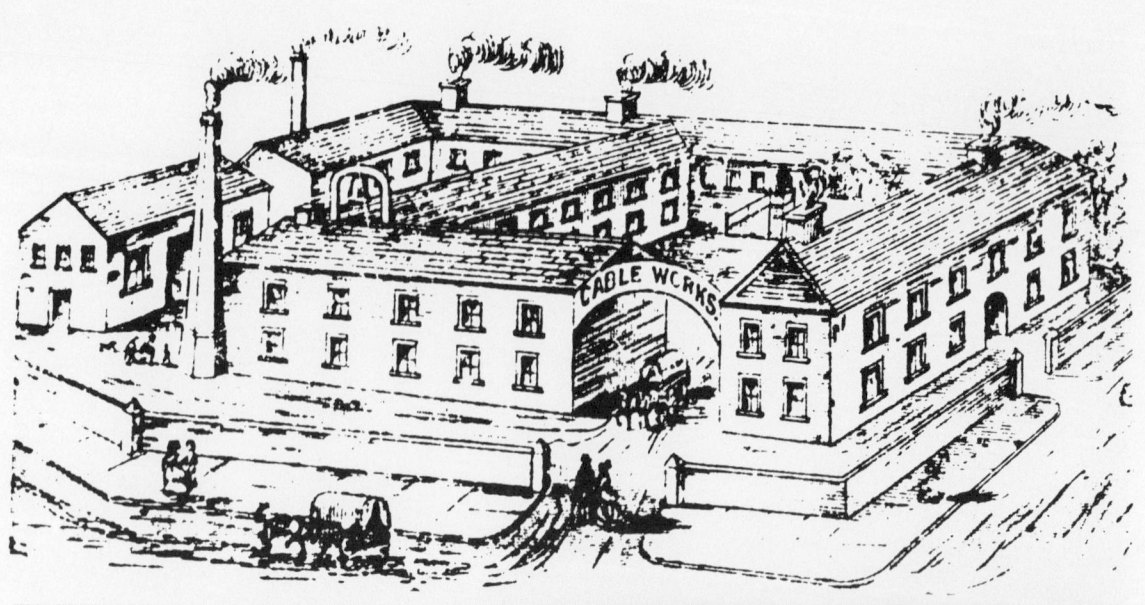

ABOVE: Cable Works, Edward Street, 1849. BELOW: Heath's Springs
Factory, Headless Cross, a typical late 19th century Redditch works famed
for precision metalwork.

Awheel and Afloat

The growth of towns during the Industrial Revolution usually depended upon the availability of coal, and on good communications. Redditch enjoyed neither. Before 1800 it would be difficult to describe Redditch as a town, for its population was only about 1,000. The Act of Parliament of 1805 for the building of the Chapel on the Green spoke of Redditch as a hamlet, but one whose population had 'of late years considerably increased'. The growth was more dramatic in the first half of the 19th century - 2,000 by 1821 and 4,500 by 1851. The needle industry became firmly established with the harnessing of steam power and the building of mills. While taking packets of needles to market did not require much more than one man on a horse, the carriage of other goods posed more serious problems. Timber was at a premium by 1800, both for fuel and as a building material. The growing town required coal and bricks and slates. It was necessary to bring much corn into Redditch: the town was not self-supporting, and high prices and shortage could lead to Bread Riots, as in 1800. Birmingham had faced similar problems in the 18th century, and had solved them by massive investment in turnpike roads and canals. On a much smaller scale, Redditch was to do the same.

Redditch had no navigable river nearer than 15 miles. The roads of Worcestershire were described in a pamphlet of 1790 as 'intolerably bad'. Indeed until 1820, the road from Redditch to Birmingham was still the old Roman Icknield Street. To reach it, traders went down Beoley Road where they forded the River Arrow. There was eventually a wooden footbridge, but the ford remained until the 1920s. It appears quite picturesque on Edwardian postcards. It was, however, dangerous. The Arrow was prone to flooding. After heavy rain, the mill owners higher up the valley opened their sluice gates to lower the level of their ponds, and a substantial amount of water came flooding down. This serious hazard to travellers is reflected in numerous accounts of the drowning of men and horses at the Beoley Road ford.

It is frequently said that John Wesley, the founder of Methodism, nearly drowned there in 1756. In his *Journal* for Monday 23 August 1756, Wesley records that he was on his way from the Black Country to Evesham. He passed through Redditch about midday. He writes that it had rained all day, and then describes a hazardous incident in which a horse nearly drowned while crossing 'a broad water'. Wesley himself 'rode through, at a small distance, very safely'. However, this episode took place some three hours' ride from Redditch on the way to Evesham. It was not at the Beoley Road ford, a few minutes' ride away. Other travellers were less fortunate.

If they survived fording the Arrow, travellers then had to use the narrow Icknield Street to the Birmingham boundary. This road ran between steep banks, and its surviving surface had been laid by Roman engineers fifteen hundred years earlier. Overtaking was difficult, passing oncoming traffic virtually impossible. Yet this was the main artery connecting the city and the little boom town of Redditch. Even as late as the 1840s, Clark's *Needle Coach* to Birmingham risked the Arrow Ford each day, using the free Icknield Street, instead of the turnpike road, which had reached Redditch in 1825.

Much of Birmingham's 18th century prosperity was due to turnpike roads. One of the busiest was the Bristol Road, which went through Bromsgrove. The nail makers of that town were able to get their produce relatively easily to the city or to the port. Industrialists from Birmingham and Redditch decided to follow suit, and to establish a turnpike trust to build a road from King's Norton *via* Alvechurch to Redditch, and thence southward into the Vale of Evesham. It was to end at Pershore and the navigable River Avon. It would enable fruit and vegetables to be brought both to Redditch and Birmingham. Redditch needles could be taken to Bristol and Birmingham.

The King's Norton — Redditch stretch of road was opened in 1825. Significantly, there was a bridge over the River Arrow by Dagnall Lane. The Trust ran into problems on the King's Norton — Birmingham stage. It would have made good sense to have used the existing Bristol Turnpike, but its trustees wanted heavy excess tolls, so it was decided to build a new road into Birmingham. In places it is barely a hundred yards from the Bristol Road: for some miles they run parallel. It retains the name Pershore Road to this day. The turnpike never did reach Pershore. The money ran out some nine miles south of Redditch, along the Ridge Way, at Dunnington Heath, where the last surviving toll house of the Pershore Road turnpike stands. The turnpike was built from capital provided by the original trustees, many of whom were needle makers. They recouped their investment from the tolls which every road user had to pay. There were toll gates at King's Norton and Dagnell Lane End, a mile to the north of Redditch. This toll house survived until the 1970s, and should have been preserved. The Ironbridge Gorge Museum has re-built one of Thomas Telford's toll cottages from his Holyhead Road, together with its gate and stretch of road surface of granite chippings, in the Blist's Hill Open Air Museum. It is regrettable that the opportunity to do the same on the Forge Mill site was missed for Redditch.

No toll was paid for use of the road within the boundaries of Redditch, but there was a second toll house at Headless Cross, roughly where the Park Inn now stands. A memory of the turnpike survives in the nearby public house called The Gate Hangs Well. No doubt the Pershore Road turnpike put Redditch on the map: it is the basis of the modern A441, but Redditch folk disliked paying tolls, and the free Icknield Street retained much traffic to and from Redditch, until the turnpike went bankrupt in the late 19th century, and the gates were kept permanently open.

More useful for the carriage of goods were canals. Birmingham invested heavily in canals in the second half of the 18th century and became the hub of the canal network of England. The Staffordshire and Worcestershire Canal connected Birmingham with the navigable River Severn at Stourport in 1772, and brought prosperity to both termini. This success led industrialists to discuss a Birmingham — Worcester Canal, which promised to be considerably shorter and therefore cheaper. It was to come within three miles of Redditch, and to play an important part in the economic history of the town.

The Worcester and Birmingham Canal Company was launched in 1789. The Act of Parliament empowering it to raise capital and begin work was passed, at considerable expense, in 1791. The survey of the route was completed by John Snape and Josiah Clowes and work began at once. The engineering of what turned out to be a difficult project was in the hands of Thomas Cartwright from 1791 to 1809, John Woodhouse from 1809 to 1811, and William Crosley from 1811 until completion. It was originally expected to cost £180,000, with funds available for a further £70,000 if necessary. In the end it cost some £610,000. The late 20th century does not have a monopoly of Concordes and Nimrods, which grossly exceed their estimated costs.

The canal from Birmingham reached the Old Wharf at Tardebigge on 30 March 1807, sixteen years after its start. It was another six years before the Tardebigge Tunnel (580 yds) was completed and the New Wharf opened. On 4 December 1815, the thirty mile stretch from Birmingham City Centre to Diglis Basin, Worcester was declared open. It had taken 24 years. The delays had been caused by the enormous expense of constructing five lengthy tunnels, and the 58 locks needed to descend the 428 feet from Tardebigge to the Severn at Worcester. The Tardebigge Tunnel was one such obstacle. It has no towpath, so narrow boats had to be legged through. While the horse was taken over the hill, two of the crew lay on a plank across the narrow boat and 'walked' it through. This could be dangerous. Men drowned in the Tardebigge Tunnel and were buried in unmarked graves in Tardebigge Churchyard. Because the tunnel was only wide enough for one boat, disputes arose between narrow boat men about precedence. They were often resolved by fisticuffs in the field by Tardebigge Church.

Redditch made use of both Old and New Wharfs at Tardebigge. The tolls on the canal were kept deliberately low to undercut competition from other Birmingham — Severn navigations. Redditch found it relatively inexpensive to use the canal for coal and corn, and the unmade roads from the wharves were soon clogged with lumbering waggons. The two most important routes were Brockhill Lane to the Old Wharf, or by the top road to the New Wharf, where the Foxlydiate Inn was profitably situated for frustrated carters. Coal rapidly replaced wood as fuel in Redditch. It was also used in the making of bricks. The local red clay was admirably suited for brickmaking and a number of works were opened. The largest, the Ferney Hill Company, using a site just off the Bromsgrove Road, continued brick making until well into the 20th century. The predominant red of the town's buildings in the past hundred and fifty years was due to the local bricks, made with canal-brought coal.

Tardebigge was the summit of the Worcester and Birmingham Canal. So great were the difficulties foreseen in preserving the water supply at Tardebigge that, at one stage, completion of the route to Worcester was planned as a railed way. Then the Company experimented with a canal lift at Tardebigge. The engineer, John Woodhouse, built his 12 foot lift where the Top Lock is now situated. The ingenious device, operated by two men, was built in 1808 and tested regularly over the next four years. It could raise or lower a boat in 2¼ minutes, and once passed 110 boats in a trial lasting twelve hours. Regrettably it was abandoned and replaced by a 14 foot deep lock, the first and deepest of the impressive Tardebigge flight. The problem of keeping water at the summit was solved by the construction of a reservoir to the south of Top Lock, and the installation of a massive Boulton and Watt steam engine to pump water into the lock. The reservoir survives as a mecca for fisherman, both human and feathered. The engine house has lost its engine, but retains its existence as a public house and night club in the somewhat unlikely setting of rural Worcestershire. The canal gradually ceased to have any economic importance after 1840, unable to compete with the railways. Even so, goods were still loaded and unloaded at Tardebigge until the 1940s. The Worcester and Birmingham Canal is now much used by pleasure craft, the Tardebigge Flight seen as a challenge rather than a hindrance to passage. There can be few pleasanter walks than down the tow path from Tardebigge New Wharf, with locks and bridges every few hundred yards, and glorious views over rural Worcestershire to the distant Malvern and Abberley Hills. It is difficult to imagine the canal as the economic life-line for an emerging industrial town — as it clearly was from 1807 to 1859, when the railway, at last, reached Redditch.

Just as the turnpike road and the canal affected Redditch later than most places, so the railway was also late. Birmingham had been connected to Manchester and Liverpool in the 1830s and to London by the end of the decade. The Birmingham and Gloucester Railway was completed by 1840, reaching the city by the famous Lickey Incline from Bromsgrove. It came no nearer Redditch than Barnt Green, but by 1844 a regular coach service from the Unicorn Inn brought Redditch rail passengers as quickly as possible to this, their nearest station.

It was in 1858 that work began on a branch line from Barnt Green *via* Alvechurch to Redditch. The Redditch Railway Company, to be taken over by the Midland Railway, built the 4½ mile stretch of line. The Hon Robert Windsor Clive MP, of the Plymouth family from Hewell Grange, inaugurated the work with a sod-turning ceremony on the site of the Redditch Railway Station on

Thursday 5 August 1858. A procession made its way from the Unicorn Inn to the site, in what is now Clive Road. They partook of a cold collation and dessert: they were charged five shillings and they paid extra for wine. A year later, passenger trains began running from 19 September, with goods services from 1 October 1859. The first issue of a local newspaper, the *Redditch Indicator*, had the news as its lead story, and carried advertisements for the first excursion, to remote and fashionable Cheltenham.

The Barnt Green — Redditch railway was single track though, as was common in the 19th century, the bridges were all double track width. During the 1860s work proceeded south of Redditch to connect the town with Alcester, Evesham and Ashchurch on the main Birmingham — Bristol line. The project was not completed until 4 May 1868. The delay was largely caused by the building of a tunnel beneath Mount Plesant. It ought to have been possible for the line to have skirted the east of Redditch and thus avoided the expense of a tunnel. But this would have involved a station some distance from the town centre — so the existing line was extended beyond the Clive Road station, and a tunnel had to be built. To save costs, it was built for single line working. A new station was erected at its northern end. Had the tunnel been wide enough for double track, Redditch might have found itself on the main line from Birmingham to London *via* Evesham and the Thames Valley. A great opportunity was missed here, and Redditch was to be served for slightly less than a century by a single track branch line, to the Vale of Evesham and beyond.

Despite its economic and social importance in the 19th and early 20th centuries, such a line was bound to suffer serious decline in the age of the motor vehicle. In 1962 and 1963, services to the south of Redditch were ended and the track was lifted. The infamous Beeching Axe of 1963 was poised above the Barnt Green — Redditch line, but the designation of Redditch as a New Town in 1964 saved it. It was needed to bring to Redditch the enormous amount of building material and road stone which New Town development would require.

The doubling of the population of Redditch between 1964 and 1985 increased the demand for passenger services between Redditch and Birmingham. With generous subsidies from the County Councils of Hereford and Worcester and of the West Midlands, British Rail increased the number of trains from a mere two a day to a regular hourly service in the 1980s. Increasing demand, aided by advertising and promotional campaigns, a railway passengers' pressure group, and a large number of successful chartered train trips, should ensure the long term future of the Redditch railway.

Until the advent of the Redditch Development Corporation in 1964, Redditch had not been well served for communications. It had no navigable river: its only turnpike road arrived as late as 1825 and ended nowhere in particular long before Pershore was reached: its railway was a late single track branch line. Had the staple industry of the town been bulkier than needles and fish hooks perhaps the story would have been different. Doubtless the Government expressed its reservations about the seriously inadequate communications of the area before it designated Redditch as a New Town. The author still recalls his first visit to the town in 1965 along a narrow sunken country track from Warwick, when there were more birds on the road than there were vehicles. He was told that the rush hour in Redditch merely meant three cars at the traffic lights instead of the usual one. All this has changed in the past twenty years. Major improvements have been made to the roads leading to Redditch, especially the building of a dual carriageway to Bromsgrove and the M5 motorway. The new roads within the designated New Town area have been built to motorway specification and — provided you can find your way — are the envy of most other towns of similar size. The completion of the M42 motorway in 1986 ensures that Redditch has immediate access to the major Midland motorways. The Development Corporation has advertised Redditch as 'The Hub of England'. Only within the past few years has this been remotely true. The good communications the town now enjoys have done much to guarantee the success of Redditch New Town. They augur well for its future into the 21st century — provided the oil does not run out.

LEFT: The Foxlydiate public house c1870. RIGHT: Turnpike cottage, Dunnington Heath, where the Pershore toll road came to its end. BELOW: The Arrow ford and footbridge, Beoley Road, 1906.

ABOVE: Toll house at Dagnell End, north of Redditch, on the Birmingham-Redditch-Pershore turnpike. LEFT: The tunnel mouth, Tardebigge New Wharf. RIGHT: The Engine House, Tardebigge. BELOW: The New Wharf, Tardebigge on the Birmingham-Worcester Canal.

Presented with the "REDDITCH INDICATOR," July 1st, 1861.

REDDITCH RAILWAY.

TIME TABLE FROM JULY THE FIRST UNTIL FURTHER NOTICE.

Trains leave	WEEK DAYS.						SUNDAYS.			
	1 2 and GOV. A.M.	1 and 2 CLASS A.M.	1 and 2 CLASS P.M.	1 and 2 CLASS P.M.	1 and 2 CLASS P.M.	1 2 and GOV. P.M.	1 2 and GOV. A.M.	1 2 and GOV. A.M.	1 2 and GOV. P.M.	1 2 and GOV. P.M.
REDDITCH	8, 20	10,* 0	1, 25	2, 30	5, 0	*7, 25	7, 0	10, 10	5, 10	8, 40
Alvechurch	8, 29	10. 9	1, 34	2, 39	5, 9	7, 34	7, 9	10, 19	5, 19	8, 49
Barnt Green, arr.	8, 35	10, 15	1, 40	2, 45	5, 15	7, 40	7, 15	10, 25	5, 25	8, 55
Arrive at Bham.	9, 20	10, 50	2, 35	3, 25	6. 0	8, 35	...	11, 15	...	9, 45
„ Worcester	...	11, 30	2, 35	...	6. 17	8, 48	8, 15	...	6, 25	...

Trains leave	WEEK DAYS.						SUNDAYS.			
	1 2 and GOV. A.M.	1 and 2 CLASS A.M.	1 and 2 CLASS P.M	1 and 2 CLASS P M	1 and 2 CLASS P.M.	1 2 and GOV. P.M.	1 2 and GOV. A.M.	1 2 and GOV. A.M.	1 2 and GOV. P.M.	1 2 and GOV. P.M.
Birmingham	7, 5	10, 5	§1, 20	...	5, 15	7, 10	6, 45	...	5, 0	...
Worcester ...	7, 44	9. 28	...	3, 5	4, 40	7, 10	...	9, 50	...	8, 20
Barnt Green ...	8, 45	10, 40	1, 50	2. 55	5, 45	8, 0	7, 25	10, 40	5, 40	9, 10
Alvechurch ...	8, 51	10, 46	1, 56	3, 1	5, 51	8, 6	7, 31	10, 46	5, 46	9, 16
Arrive at Redditch	9, 0	10, 55	‡2, 5	3, 10	6, 0	8, 15	7, 40	10, 55	5, 55	9, 25

* ALCESTER & STUDLEY.—An Omnibus leaves Alcester calling at Studley every Week-day in time to meet the Trains leaving Redditch at 10,0 a.m. and 5,0 p.m., and returns from Redditch after the arrival of Trains leaving Birmingham at 10.5 a.m., and 5,15 p.m.

Third Class with all trains between Redditch and Birmingham.

§A Train leaves Birmingham for Barnt Green at 1.0 p.m., but does not go on to Redditch until the next, arriving 2,5 p.m.

*These two carry mails out. ‡ This one brings a mail in.

LEFT: The Top Lock of the Tardebigge flight on the Birmingham-Worcester Canal. RIGHT: The single track Redditch Railway, with double width bridges. BELOW: Redditch railway timetable, 1861.

ABOVE: Railway Station, Redditch and BELOW: looking south, both c1920.

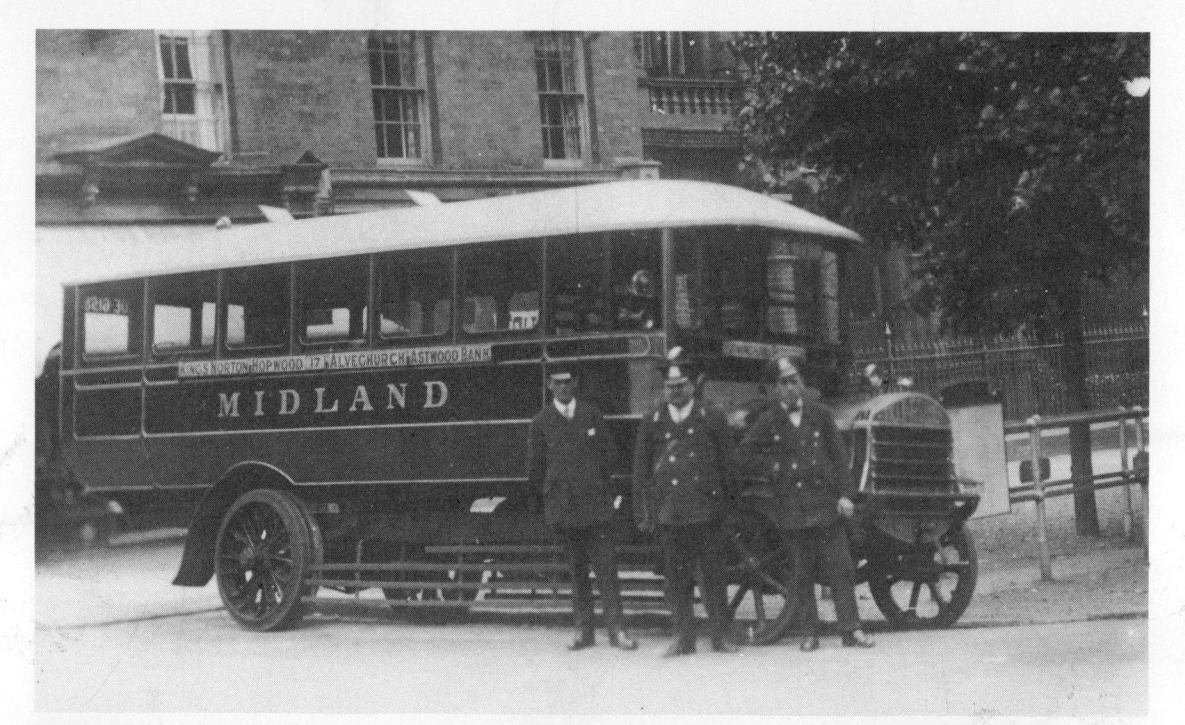

ABOVE: Midland Red Birmingham-Redditch-Astwood Bank 'bus and crew, 1920. BELOW: The first Midland Red double decker 'buses to be used in Redditch, 1 March 1936.

LEFT: William Avery, first historian of Redditch, 1885. RIGHT: Alcester Street and the old lock-up, c1880. BELOW: The old lock-up, popularly called The Hole, built in 1824 at the junction of Alcester Street and Red Lion Street.

Industrious and Diligent

It was during the 19th century that Redditch became a place of some consequence. Described as a hamlet in 1805, Redditch appears on no maps of Worcestershire before 1775, and only occasionally thereafter. At the time of the first census in 1801, the population was about 1,000. A high birthrate and considerable immigration from rural Worcestershire and Warwickshire, caused by the booming needle industry, doubled the population in twenty years. A number of migrations of needle makers from elsewhere, the most striking being the arrival in the town of the Long Crendon needle makers from Buckinghamshire, led to continuous expansion. By 1851 there were 4,500 people living in Redditch: ten years later there were 5,500 and in 1871, 6,700. The large increases thereafter are, in part, explained by the inclusion of outlying areas such as Upper Ipsley, Ipsley Webheath and Feckenham. In 1901 the population was 13,493. By 1931 it had reached 19,281. The increase in the 1930s was a steady one, with a significant immigration from South Wales. By 1951 the town had 28,877 inhabitants and, on the eve of Redditch being declared a New Town in 1964, the population had reached 35,000.

The description of Redditch in 1776, written by Joseph Monk many years later, and quoted earlier, shows a small community living around the Green and on three roads running from it. It was so small that Monk could remember everyone's name and where they lived. It was a village with no place of worship apart from a Quaker Meeting House, which flourished from 1704 to 1796, and the Gatehouse Chapel, which Monk did not mention since it did not fall within his perambulation of Redditch.

William Avery, a Headless Cross needle maker, who produced the first history of the town in 1887, must have relied upon family memories when he too described those who lived around the Green in the early 19th century. He could not resist libelling John George as 'the head grocer who sanded his sugar' nor Tim Munslow 'who manufactured cakes and mutton pies which he carried round on Saturday nights to the public houses for sale, and warmed them up every subsequent Saturday till they were disposed of'. Tim Munslow could do no wrong, however, for he had achieved one moment of immortality — he had shod the horse of the Duke of Wellington on the eve of Waterloo.

Avery also records extracts from an unpublished directory of Redditch, written in 1822 by Frederick Milward. The people 'are in general very industrious and diligent. The girls are very beautiful, particularly in their complexions and figures, rendered more so by their flowing and costly dresses . . .' Later, published directories are much less flattering — and less interesting.

Like many similar industrial towns, there was a violent side to early 19th century Redditch. It had a reputation for producing prize-fighters. Tom Paddock, the 'Redditch Needle Pointer' was the bare knuckle champion of England in 1855, before losing in the following year to the 'Tipton Slasher'. A field in Crabbs Cross, known locally as Boney's Island, behind the Star and Garter public house, was popular as a venue for prize-fighting, since it was on the border of Worcestershire and Warwickshire, and spectators could escape the local magistrates by rapidly crossing the county boundary. The White Hart at Headless Cross was another venue for the Fancy in the 1820s. The reputation of Redditch fighting men was often put to the test by the navvies building the canal at Tardebigge. On one occasion, a major fracas occurred at Foxlydiate Wake, when forty navvies took on a Redditch group. History does not record the verdict — only that the navvies had to resort to weapons. It is not surprising that a small gaol was built in the town in 1824. It was politely called the Old Lock-up, and more commonly The Hole. It was on the corner of Alcester Street and Red Lion Street. Significantly, it was the town's first public building!

As brutal as prize fighting, bull baiting was also a common pastime. The Star and Garter field at Crabbs Cross was still being used as late as 1829 for spectacles lasting all day, with a tethered bull baited by individual dogs. At the day's end, the exhausted bull was set upon by all the surviving dogs. On occasions the bull escaped and charged the crowd. William Avery records how a cripple was completely cured of his disability when faced by an enraged and injured bull. He threw his crutches away and ran for safety! Doubtless dogs and bulls were less lucky. Cock fighting was also practised in Redditch. An attempt to raise the tone slightly, by introducing horse racing, was made in 1838, and for some forty years there was a small race course off Beoley Road, by the banks of the Arrow.

Redditch men could be as unpleasant to other human beings as they were to animals. It was regarded as fair game to pour *dotment* or factory grease over the head of any pedlar arriving in the town — just in case he might dare to sell cheap needles, not made locally. A pedlar who objected to this treatment was pulled through the factory mill pond so that the grease set. William Avery was pleased to record in 1887 that such practical jokes were things of the past, 'now that civilisation and good sense have taken Redditch into their course'.

Some of the credit for the spread of civilisation is due to the work of the churches in the town. The Church of England opened their Chapel on the Green in 1808 and had to extend it, by adding galleries, in 1816 and 1827. Unbelievably, it held a congregation of 1,000. A succession of curates from Tardebigge served it in its early years, but it was Rev John Clayton, Curate from 1820 to 1842, and Rev George Fessey, Curate and then Vicar from 1842 to 1884 who turned it into a well-attended church. The Worcestershire antiquarian, John Noake, paid a visit to the Chapel in 1850, describing all he saw in one of the volumes of *The Rambler* (1851). Though he thought the Chapel 'an architectural abortion', he found 'the inhabitants of Redditch a God-fearing people'. The Chapel was 'filled by one of the most respectable, decently behaved congregations I have ever seen'. Other remarkable features of the service were that 'with few exceptions, no one slept during the sermon' and the babies and young children behaved themselves. In the Religious Census of 1851, a fifth of the population of Redditch attended a church service. The Chapel on the Green and, from 1855, St Stephen's Church, presented the only Anglican presence in the town until 1876, when St George's Church (Architect, G.E. Preedy) was opened to serve the needs of the growing population of the Beoley Road area. The Church of St Luke in Headless Cross was built in 1843 and rebuilt in 1867/8.

The Methodists seem to have shown greater enterprise than the Anglicans. John Wesley visited Redditch on three occasions, preaching on Thursday 12 March 1761, 'to a deeply serious congregation', but it was not until 1806 that plans were set in motion to establish a mission to Redditch. The Superintendent of the Birmingham Circuit, Rev Richard Reece, wrote to the Secretary of the Missionary Committee in London: '. . . to introduce the Methodist Gospel . . . I have already a list of twelve places where it is probable a door will be opened for the Gospel if a suitable person be appointed. One of them I will mention: Redditch. Containing a population of 2000. No religious worship amongst them. The trade, needle making. There was a Chapel of Ease, but it has been long unfit for use and now they are begun to build another . . . in no part of England is a missionary more needed, nor could he be employed anywhere with greater probability of success'.

Reece proved to be correct. A missionary, possibly James Eaton, was sent, and services began in the house of a Mr Turner on Breedon (now Ipsley Street or Beoley Road West). By 1808 a small chapel had been built. Rowney Green opened its Chapel in 1809 and Crabbs Cross three years later. By 1810 Redditch was a Methodist Circuit with two ministers. Their work was not always peaceful. Services were disrupted. On one occasion, the vigorous action of Mrs Turner restored peace, when a band of hooligans with fife, drum and pans was making worship impossible. The formidable Mrs Turner came out of Chapel brandishing a knife, which she promptly put through the drum, thus putting the Devil to flight. The Breedon congregation is also recorded as having beaten up a group of persecutors from Ipsley and Redditch, and 'a gigantic brother named John Hollington' dropped one offensive intruder down the Chapel steps. Such was the Church militant in the early 19th century.

The Methodists rapidly expanded their activities. Breedon Chapel was extended in 1817. Methodists began worship in Headless Cross in 1820 at the house now numbered 44, Birchfield Road. The tendency for Methodists to splinter into sects was evident in Redditch. The Primitive Methodists arrived in 1830 with John Tharm, 'a mighty man of God', having an effective mission in 1834. A Primitive Methodist Chapel was opened in Adelaide Street in 1839, and another in Headless Cross in 1867. When the former proved too small, the Alcester Street Chapel was opened in 1890. By the end of the century the Wesleyan Methodists were strongly established at Bates Hill Church, opened in 1843 (with an inaugural collection of over £200), and extended in 1881. The United Free Methodists had a chapel at the junction of Evesham Street and Ludlow Road — surviving today as the WRVS Day Centre. In Headless Cross, the Wesleyans built their first Chapel on Evesham Road in 1827, replacing it in 1858 and again in 1873. It was this Church which was destroyed by an extraordinarily ferocious gale which did much damage in Redditch in 1895. On Sunday 24 March, shortly after the caretaker had left the building, the wind lifted the roof of the Church and, within a matter of minutes, the building had collapsed. It is some tribute to the strength and wealth of the Methodists in Redditch that they had the present Headless Cross Church built within a year.

The Baptists took longer to organise themselves. Though there was a congregation of Baptists in Astwood Bank in 1787, with a chapel in 1813, it was not until 1862 that a fellowship developed in Redditch. A Chapel was opened on Ipsley Street in 1868. A much grander Church was built at Pool Meadow in 1898. Somewhat surprisingly it was incorporated into the factory of Terry's Springs during the First World War. Redditch people felt that Divine wrath caused the fire which severely damaged the building in the 1920s. The Terry family provided the money for the new Baptist Church in Easemore Road.

A Congregational Church was founded in the 1820s by an enterprising needle maker called Thomas Williams. He made a small fortune and, conscious of the difficulties faced by rich men entering the Kingdom of Heaven, built a chapel onto his works and house in Evesham Street. By 1828 there was a thriving congregation, and eventually a most imposing Church and Sunday School were built. In front was what came to be known as the Needle makers' Graveyard.

The most significant event, architecturally speaking, of the 19th century church building expansion, was the opening in 1834 of the Roman Catholic Church of Our Lady of Mount Carmel on Beoley Road. Catholicism survived quite strongly after the Reformation in this area of the Midlands. A Mass House at Beoley survived the persecutions of the 17th century and the Throckmortons at Coughton Court remained loyal to the old faith. After the passage of the Catholic Relief Act of 1829, church building could begin, and the Catholic Church of Redditch may well be 'the first Gothic Catholic Church of any pretensions built in England since the Reformation'. This was what the early historian of the needle industry, Michael T. Morrall, believed — and he proudly recorded that he was the altar boy on the day of the consecration. The architect of Mount Carmel was a Quaker, Thomas Rickman, a well known student of church architecture, who has given to posterity the traditional names of church building styles — Norman, Early English, Decorated and Perpendicular. He chose a peculiar version of the latter for Mount Carmel.

Throughout the 19th century, a large proportion of the population attended these churches. Despite denominational differences, there seem to have been cooperation and friendly relations between them. There were exchanges of pulpits among the Nonconformists, but William Avery could not resist a dig at the tensions which may have existed, when he described the Coronation celebrations of Queen Victoria in 1838: '. . . and strangest of all, the Vicar and the Wesleyan minister went arm in arm amongst the people as though they were servants of the same God and believed that the injunction in the New Testament to "Love one another" was really intended to be acted upon.'

Avery was in many ways a modern character — an ecumenical organist who had played in almost all the churches in Redditch — though he owed allegiance to the Wesleyan Methodist Church at Headless Cross. What all the churches had in common were Sunday Schools and an interest in education. A large number of children attended these schools, and numerous contemporary descriptions comment favourably upon the standards reached, and the interest and good behaviour of the children. There were regular Sunday School treats, outings and sports, sometimes by train to the Lickey Hills, at other times in local fields after enormous processions all round the town. Frequently all the denominations joined in, including Anglicans and Roman Catholics, the latter being incongruously placed with the Primitive Methodists in one of the parades!

Many Redditchians must have received all their education in the Sunday Schools, for official education arrived late. It was not until 1845 that a National School was founded. St Stephen's School was built on land off what is now Peakman Street, given by the Hon Robert and Lady Harriett Clive. It was intended for poor persons from Redditch and Tardebigge. It was not very grand, consisting of two large classrooms, one for boys and one for girls, an infant's room and a school master's house. Nonetheless it fulfilled a serious need, as was evident when it opened on 23 October: 'Long before the hour fixed for dinner, the doors were besieged by young eager guests, and at the hour appointed upward of 470 children were seated round the tables, on which was placed an ample supply of roast beef and plum pudding of the best possible description cooked in a very excellent manner.'

They no longer open schools with such a flourish. St Stephen's School was enlarged in 1870 and again in 1893, and survived into the 1960s before being moved to more modern premises. Even then, the building had a further lease of life as an annexe to the College of Further Education, before demolition in 1983.

Other National Schools were built at St George's and at St Luke's, Headless Cross. After the 1870 Education Act, a Board School was opened to serve Crabbs Cross. To cater for those wanting more than an elementary education, a Redditch Technical School was started in the late 19th century. After the 1902 Education Act, this became the Redditch Secondary School, moving into new premises on Easemore Road. This building became the Technical College in 1929, when new buildings were provided a little further down Easemore Road to house the Redditch County High School. At long last the town had a grammar school. During the first half of the 20th century, those not able to gain a place at the County High School attended a variety of all-age schools, which they entered at five and left when they attained school-leaving age. The 1944 Education Act, requiring the County Council to provide secondary education for all, took many years to be fulfilled in Redditch. Bridley Moor Secondary Modern School, opened in 1952, was the first purpose-built school under the Act. It was followed by Lodge Farm, Walkwood and Ridgeway Secondary Schools later in the decade. With the County High School expanded to take secondary technical pupils as well as grammar school ones, the town had a fully operational system of secondary education by the 1960s — in time for the theorists to decide it was obsolete and ripe for reorganisation into a three-tier comprehensive system.

The mid-19th century also saw an interest in adult education. In October 1850 was founded the Redditch Literary and Scientific Institute. For a subscription of 4s, members had the use of a reading room at No 4, Prospect Hill, and access to numerous lectures of an improving nature. From 1862 Saturday evening entertainments were held, under the indefatigable William Avery, but they were discontinued six years later, when 'the tone became unsuited to the support of a Literary and Scientific Institute'. The organisation continued to fulfil a demand elsewhere, and its success was at its height in 1886 when its own premises, including a School of Art, were opened on Church Green West by Lord Beauchamp. The Institute faded away in the 20th century with the coming of a variety of other distractions, but its founders would not be too displeased to see their building still used for educational purposes, as an annexe to the College of Further Education. They would be delighted too to see that the Redditch Society, founded in 1945 as a lecture society, continues their aims of appreciating Science, Literature and Art. The Society celebrated its first forty years, with a dinner in 1985. The library of the Institute became the basis for the excellent Public Library, formerly under the care of the Urban District Council, and now administered by the County Council.

More and more of the facilities of a town arrived in Redditch from the 1850s. Some form of local government arrived in 1858 with the selection of eight Improvement Commissioners to attend to sanitation, but the following year must have seemed a major one for those eager to encourage the town's development. The Redditch Benefit Building Society (now Midshires Building Society) was founded: the *Redditch Indicator,* the town's first newspaper, was launched by William Heming: its first issue recorded the arrival of the railway. Two years later a Savings Bank was opened, and in 1862 Redditch became a Petty Sessions district with its own Magistrates' Court.

The Milwards, Bartleets, Hemings, Averys, even the Windsor-Clives, could feel proud of the remarkable progress their town had made — in almost every field except housing and public health. Here the record was appalling. Warning had been given in 1832, when a serious outbreak of cholera occurred. Some fifty people died and panic set in. The source of the outbreak was identified as Big Pool, a pond at the junction of Alcester Street and Ipsley Street, into which dead cats and dogs as well as sewage from Red Lion Street and Paoli's Row were all thrown. Panic-stricken needle makers took to brandy to drown their sorrows, and because they understood it to be a preventative. They were encouraged to do so by Dr Royston, one of three doctors in the town, who came out of the episode with credit. The good doctor, living on Prospect Hill, kept a supply of coffee, biscuits and brandy on a table in his hall, all three being available to anyone fearing the disease. The National Health Service is not so generous. The burial ground of the Gatehouse Chapel was re-opened, at first for night-time burials, but later at any time. Little time elapsed between death and burial, and there is at least one story of a victim allegedly buried alive. The family of a young lady called Ramsay, whom the doctor declared dead, prevented her burial by defending her with a pitch fork. She apparently recovered, and lived to a good old age. A day of penance was held on 21 March, and of thanksgiving when the outbreak was over, on 14 December.

Big Pool was not however filled in and further epidemics, though not of cholera, occurred. In a smallpox outbreak in 1838, the landlord of the Horse and Jockey buried five children in three weeks. Some attempt was made to provide Redditch with brick-built sewers in 1845, with a start made in Walford Street, but the enterprise soon failed. When the Improvement Commissioners began work in 1858, they found a town without sewers or a fresh water supply. Redditch had grown rapidly without any public health regulations. The need to be near one's place of work led to the building of courts of houses on any available piece of land. Back-to-back houses were as common as in northern industrial towns. Middens and cesspits were open to the elements. Houses drew their water supply from wells which, being deeper than the leaking cesspits, were contaminated by them. Little wonder that Rev G.F. Fessey at St Stephen's was burying an average of 130 people a year, most of them children. The Register for December 1844 is typical:

NAME	ABODE	DATE	AGE	MINISTER
Ann Eliza Cox	Redditch	3rd Dec	4 years	G.F. Fessey
Joseph Beard	Redditch	4th Dec	40 years	G.F. Fessey
Charles Edward Cox	Redditch	5th Dec	13 months	G.F. Fessey
Byrne Wilkes	Redditch	5th Dec	12 hours	G.F. Fessey
James William Harborne	Redditch	6th Dec	4 months	G.F. Fessey
John Crow	Redditch	7th Dec	2 yrs 10 mths	G.F. Fessey
Catherine Wilkinson	From Ipsley	12th Dec	7 months	G.F. Fessey
Richard Bint	Redditch	17th Dec	10 months	G.F. Fessey
Owen Louch	Redditch	17th Dec	2½ years	G.F. Fessey
Sarah Ann Wilkinson	From Ipsley	18th Dec	3 yrs 6 mths	G.F. Fessey
George Bartleet James	Redditch	22nd Dec	1 yr 8 mths	G.F. Fessey
William Edwin Perks	Redditch	25th Dec	7 months	G.F. Fessey
Sarah Elizabeth Johnson	Redditch	27th Dec	4 months	G.F. Fessey

A sewerage scheme was finally proposed in 1868, but it was to cost £10,700, so it was abandoned. However, the Public Health Act of 1875 forced a Local Board of Health upon a reluctant town. The eight members selected Dr Herbert Page as their Medical Officer of Health, and had the courage to have his report for the year 1875 printed and published. He described the physique of the population as 'that of a manufacturing district . . . with stature short, or seldom above average and countenance pallid'. His description of town centre housing defies belief: 'water in cellars, dampness of walls, penetration of roofs by water, want of glazing, smallness of rooms, broken quarried floors, filthy condition of houses, saturation of subsoil around the dwellings, unwholesome, inadequate or absence of water supply, wretchedly constructed closets . . . the midden often found in its worst form, open, undrained, half full of decomposing house sulliage.' 332 people had no access to a lavatory: others were shared by an average of forty people. Only ⅓ of the 700 middens in the towns were covered as the law required. Only 1/7 of the streets of Redditch were adequately sewered. Out of 40 streets, 23 were completely without sewers. Dr Page wrote: 'I deem the provision of a complete and proper sewage system for the district an absolute and pressing necessity'. No less a priority was the provision of a fresh water supply. Dr Page discovered that 218 people, living in 58 houses, had no water supply at all. Headless Cross, despite being out in the country, was little better, over a hundred people having no closet, and 81 no access to a water supply.

Dr Page's report unleashed a furore. The cost of an adequate sewerage scheme — a re-assessment of the 1868 scheme by Gott and Beasley of London — had risen to £15,600. The ratepayers were up in arms. The columns of the *Redditch Indicator* were filled with letters from ratepayers, who clearly did not suffer from the abuses Dr Page had described. A Ratepayers' Association was founded to fight the proposed sewerage and water schemes. Men of some standing in the community described the proposed expenditure as 'excessive and unnecessary'. Richard Hemming 'did not consider anything of the kind necessary'. Edmund Holyoake saw no necessity for either sewerage or water supply. They seized eagerly on Dr Page's admission that the death rate in Redditch was, astonishingly, below the national average.

The ratepayers and their petitions and public meetings kept a brake on the efforts of the Local Board, who were declared 'a defaulting authority' in 1879. The sewerage scheme was not begun until 1881. In the following year the East Worcestershire Waterworks Company opened its Burcot Pumping Station, and pipes were laid to Headless Cross, where an underground reservoir and a water tower were constructed and Redditch people had access, at last, to pure water. In celebration, Mr R.S. Bartleet presented the town with a cast-iron fountain, which he was alleged to have designed himself and which his wife unveiled on 15 May 1883. Its allegorical female figure represented the supplier of fresh water, as well as promoting Temperance, a favourite cause of Mr Bartleet. The fountain was restored and repainted by Redditch Development Corporation in time for its centenary.

The arrival of piped water was only a partial solution to the public health scandal. The Ratepayers' Association continued to campaign against heavy rates, demanding the resignation of the Local Board in 1886. It is difficult to sympathise with those individuals who opposed expenditure on such necessities as proper sanitation; it is equally difficult to support the Local Board, who for so long failed to give the highest priority to the provision of sewers. Sixteen years after Dr Page's horrific report, the *Redditch News*, an ephemeral journal of 1891, ran a series on 'Insanitary Redditch', which is, incredibly, more appalling than anything he described.

The intrepid journalist on the *News* regarded Clarke's Yard as at least as bad as any slum in Whitechapel or Bethnal Green, but reserved his strictest comments for Silver Street, a slum between Red Lion Street and George Street.

'Silver Street is a curiously shaped thoroughfare, part of it resembling a square, and part a long narrow lane. The ground all through was littered over, not merely with refuse of all kinds but with human excreta, for which apparently, there was no other place. At one end of the street there are three privies to six houses — two of which are lodging houses, one licensed for twelve and the other for thirty lodgers . . . one privy is in a most dilapidated condition, the door off the hinges, the roof leaky, the wall broken, the seat in fragments, the whole place foul and pestilential, and this has to serve for either two or three houses.'

Conditions in Easemore Lane, Orchard Street, Herbert Street and the notorious Warren's Buildings were equally disgraceful. Unicorn Hill 'not altogether an Arcadia', had 'an enormous heap of manure, enclosed within two walls, within 9 feet 6 inches of a dwelling house . . . stinking most foully, even in winter'. Stung by the criticisms, the Local Board agreed that the abuses were 'a disgrace to the town'. In a letter to the paper, signed by four nonconformist ministers, conditions were described as 'a danger to health and morals'. The newspaper summarised the abuses in 1891 under six headings — unpaved courts and yards, surface pollution caused by the dirtiness of the tenants and the lack of refuse receptacles, insufficient closet accommodation, filthy middens and privies, the accumulation of manure and garbage, and the keeping of animals next door to houses. It is astonishing to read such descriptions of a small town within a few minutes' walk of beautiful Worcestershire countryside. The new Urban District Council, established in 1894, clearly had a major task on its hands, and it was well into the 20th century before the abuses were cleared away.

It is not surprising that a Redditch which appeared to care so little for public health had more than its share of poverty. At the beginning of the 19th century, the relief of poverty was still in the hands of the elected Overseers of the Poor administering the Elizabethan Poor Law system. These officers collected rates and gave grants of money to those in need. The paying-out book for the parish of Ipsley from 1797 to 1804 has fortunately survived in the County Record Office, showing how the poor were cared for in about half of our area. Each year a different Overseer was elected. It does not seem to have been a popular office: the poor certainly required much hard work and attention to detail. The Overseer appears to have spent part of every day handing out small sums of money to those who asked.

Ipsley gives every impression in those years of being a rural parish virtually unaffected by the Industrial Revolution. The problems of enclosure, inflation, poverty and the misery of the Napoleonic Wars loom large. Whereas the first recorded Overseer, William Sheward, disbursed £259 in 1797 and had to collect the rates quarterly, his successor in 1801 gave out over £800 and had to collect twelve instalments of the rates. The payments were often small — sixpence or a shilling a day — and were frequently paid out day after day, week after week. William Sable appears regularly throughout the seven years of the book. In the early entries he appears as Sabel, with no christian name, and he is regularly given a shilling. By 1801, it appears he was married, and his wife was given 10 yards of cloth and a pair of blankets. In March, Ann, his wife, had her spinning wheel repaired from the rates, and later on he had his shoes mended, at a cost of three shillings. This was roughly the amount he was given weekly in June and July when he was ill. During the autumn and winter, he was given an axe and a hundred weight of coal. In 1802 they had a child and they clearly struggled to keep the child both warm and alive. There were regular small payments for coal, and because the child was ill. The Sable home must have been a miserable affair for, in 1803, the new Overseer, William Cope, provided two hundred bricks and some lime for repairs, and a builder called Whitehouse put in two day's work repairing the house. Unfortunately, the paying-out book ends in 1804, and William and Ann Sable disappear from history. The system of poor relief, administered by relatively generous and understanding local men, who clearly lived among the poor, appears well-suited to the small rural community of Ipsley, though the ratepayers may have thought otherwise.

It was less useful in rapidly expanding industrial towns. Whereas Ipsley appears peaceful in the crisis years covered by the Overseers' Book, Redditch temporarily suffered a collapse of law and order. On 9 May 1800 a starving crowd attacked the bread shops of Redditch and the local constable and magistrates lost control. As was usual in the days before a regular police force, the County Militia were sent for — in this case, a group of part-time soldiers from Bromsgrove. They proved utterly incapable of subduing the Redditch riot, their discomfort and retreat being described in verse by the Bromsgrove poet John Crane who, as a member of the Bromsgrove Volunteers, played an inglorious part in the incident:

> 'The siege of Redditch, I was there all the while,
> With nothing to eat but a piece of a tile;
> Men, women and children, with trade all alive,
> Clods, pebbles and brickbats sent at us full drive.
> Sent at us on purpose to batter our pates
> Tongs, shovels and pokers, and cheeks of old grates;
> A line of stout women, with ladles three deep,
> Determined to drive us, or send us to sleep.
> The leader well armed with a stout wooden crutch,
> Ten women to one Bromsgrove man, is too much.
> The sun sunk away at the sight of the fun
> The moon at the brightest, to light us to run.
> When quarrels are up to a terrible pitch,
> Be off, like a Crane, from the siege of Redditch.
> I'm singing of sieges, your chance is but small,
> The siege of Redditch is the flogger of all.'

Such riots were not uncommon in the early 19th century and a series in 1830 throughout England, which included an incident in Redditch in December, convinced the Whig Government that the expensive Elizabethan Poor Law would have to be amended. By an Act of Parliament of 1834, outdoor relief was ended, parishes were grouped together into Unions, and relief would only be given inside a workhouse. The parish of Tardebigge, which still contained most of Redditch, was made part of the Bromsgrove Union, whose Board of Guardians first met in 1836. They quickly agreed to build a Workhouse to serve the Union on Gravel Pit Piece, to the north of Bromsgrove. They equally quickly agreed that the old and infirm might have tea instead of gruel, because it would be less expensive. They appointed a firm of architects called Bateman and Drury to design a Workhouse for 300 paupers — because their estimate was £700 cheaper than their nearest rival. In 1837 the Board of Guardians sent a 'Humble Petition' to the House of Lords, commending the Poor Law Amendment Act of 1834 because it afforded 'more effectual relief to the really necessitous and removed those inducements to idleness and pauperism which notoriously existed under the Old

System'. The builders of the Workhouse, struggling to keep costs down within the estimate, went bankrupt and the building was not opened until March 1839. It remained the Workhouse for Redditch and the surrounding area until 1948. It survives today as All Saints Hospital, Bromsgrove.

For ninety years the poor, the old, the unemployed and the sick had to trudge six or seven miles to be subjected to investigation, compulsory bathing, de-lousing and separation from family, and to enjoy bread, cheese, gruel, suet pudding and occasional meat. For the past forty years, latter day Redditchians have gone to the same building to give birth, to receive treatment, to be operated upon and perhaps to die. It was not until 1895 that Redditch had its own hospital. This was a small cottage hospital, the campaign for which was begun by William Avery in 1865. It was suggested in 1887 that a hospital be built as a permanent memorial for Queen Victoria's Golden Jubilee. In the end two successful needle makers, William and Edwin Smallwood, provided the money, and the hospital was built. Despite extensions, it was seriously inadequate for the town by the mid-20th century. Though it was possible to die at the Smallwood Hospital, no Redditch baby could be born there in recent years — and accidents could only be treated in office hours. When the new District Hospital is opened in 1986, the campaign for it will have lasted about as long as Avery's.

When the 20th century dawned, Redditch was a changing place. The needle industry no longer had a monopoly. While the number of needles made per week remained colossal, the number of firms was declining. There was some diversification of industry before the First World War. It was not difficult to change from needles and fish hooks to springs and other light metal goods. It was no great leap either from parts for bicycles to making bicycles. By 1914 Redditch was producing the famous Royal Enfield motorcycles. Diversification of industry continued during the inter-war period — and probably saved Redditch from suffering too badly from the mass unemployment of the period. The town was relatively prosperous, no longer relying on one basic industry, and there was migration into Redditch by those seeking work, especially from South Wales.

The initiative and energy of the industrialists of the town may best be exemplified by the extraordinary story of the meeting at the Unicorn Hotel in 1919 of a British engineer and a Swedish battery designer who, between them, using a Swedish-English dictionary as a business aid, founded a firm, eventually to become Chloride-Alcad Batteries. The Manchester University-trained engineer was Mr G. Scott Atkinson, who spent six days a week travelling as far as London and Newcastle, taking orders for the new dry batteries, and the seventh on doing his paper work. From a work force of two, the firm expanded rapidly, taking over the former Enfield Motor Cycle Works at Hunt End. No less dramatic was the growth of such firms as Hydrovane Limited, making compressors, and High Duty Alloys, who established themselves on Windsor Road, just before the outbreak of the Second World War, in time to play a major part in the development of the vital aircraft industry. The siting of this huge factory in Redditch was caused as much by its remoteness from German bombs as by the metallurgical skills of the townspeople.

Redditch escaped lightly from German bombing and carried on after 1945 much as it had done before. Enormous changes had taken place between 1800, when Redditch was little more than a hamlet, and 1945, when it was an important manufacturing centre. Those changes were as nought compared to what was to happen in the next forty years.

ABOVE: Alcester Street, c1905. BELOW: Methodism in Headless Cross 1820-1897: CENTRE: No 44 Birchfield Road, where Methodists began worship 1820 and RIGHT: Wesleyan Chapel, Headless Cross, 1827. BELOW: Methodist Chapel, 1873, destroyed by a gale (1895) and Headless Cross Methodist Church in 1897. The three paintings were probably by J.M. Woodward. They were presented to Headless Cross Methodist Church in memory of William Avery.

LEFT: Alcester Street Primitive Methodist Chapel, 1898. RIGHT: Bates Hill Wesleyan Methodist Church, opened 1843. CENTRE: Primitive Methodist Junior Christian Endeavour Class, 1910. BELOW: The Baptist Church at Ipsley Green, once the site of the notorious Town Pool. The Church was taken over by Terry's works during the 1914-18 war.

ABOVE: Baptist Chapel and Sunday School, Astwood Bank, late 19th century. BELOW: The King's Arms and Mount Carmel RC Church, c1870.

LEFT: St Luke's Church, Headless Cross, c1910. RIGHT: St George's Church, 1876, (architect: G.E. Preedy). BELOW: Redditch housing in the 19th century.

OPPOSITE ABOVE: St Stephen's National Schools, opened 1845, engraved by W.T. Heming. CENTRE: Staff of St Stephen's National School, 1902. BELOW: The Redditch County High School, opened in 1929 · ABOVE: Crabbs Cross School: Class 2 Boys, c1914. LEFT: Redditch Secondary School, Easemore Road. (now the Abbey High School). RIGHT: The Literary and Scientific Institute opened by Lord Beauchamp in 1886. Originally a centre for adult education, the building later served as the School of Art and the town's library. It is today an annexe of the College of Further Education.

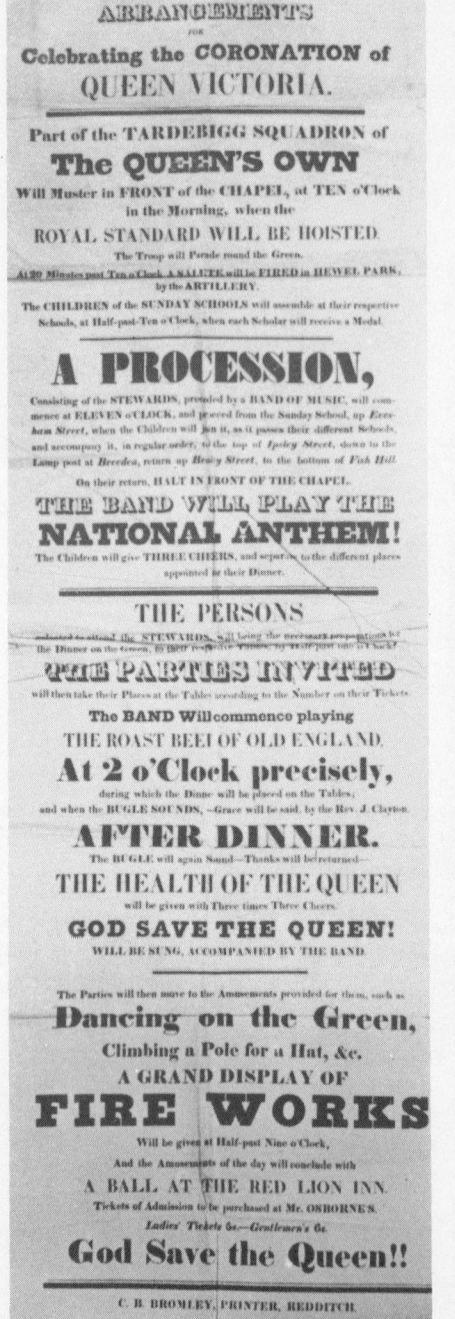

LEFT: Poster for celebrations for Queen Victoria's Coronation, June 1838.
RIGHT: The Bartleet Fountain (1883) commemorating the provision of a
fresh water supply for Redditch. Cast at the Coalbrookdale Company's works
in Shropshire.

ABOVE: The Ivy House and Post Office, Church Green West. The post-mistress in the mid-19th century was Miss Elizabeth Taylor. BELOW: The Bromsgrove Union Workhouse, opened 1838, which served the Redditch area.

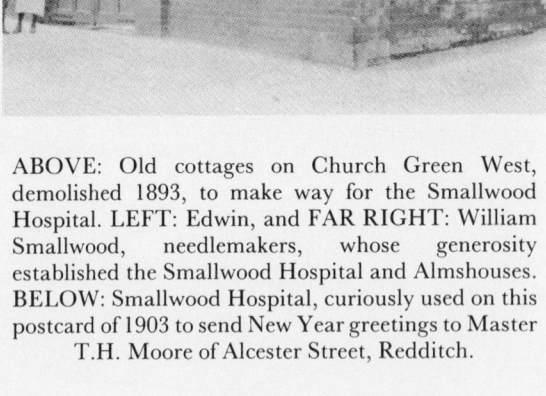

ABOVE: Old cottages on Church Green West, demolished 1893, to make way for the Smallwood Hospital. LEFT: Edwin, and FAR RIGHT: William Smallwood, needlemakers, whose generosity established the Smallwood Hospital and Almshouses. BELOW: Smallwood Hospital, curiously used on this postcard of 1903 to send New Year greetings to Master T.H. Moore of Alcester Street, Redditch.

ABOVE: Opening of Smallwood Hospital 1895, attended by Lord and Lady Windsor, the Bishop of Coventry and Austen Chamberlain MP. BELOW: The Smallwood Almshouses, the second of the gifts to the town by the Smallwood brothers.

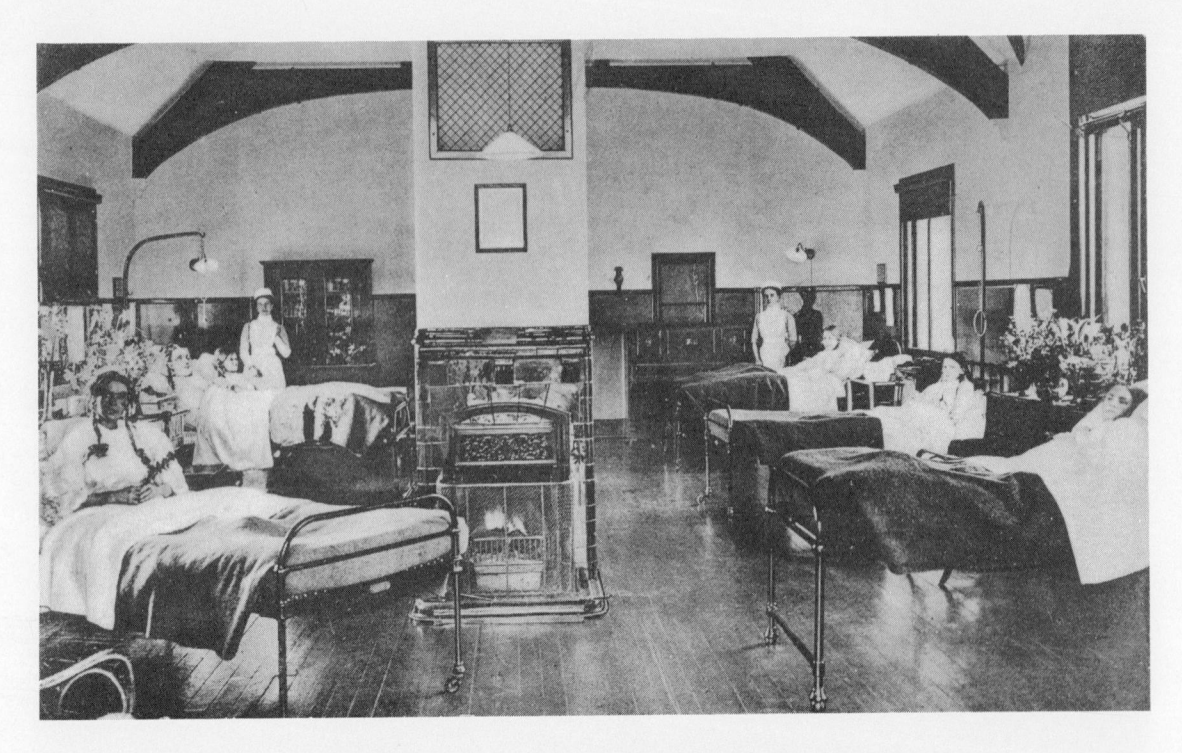

ABOVE: Female Ward, Smallwood Hospital 1914. BELOW: Royal Enfield
Cycle Works, Hewell Road.

ABOVE: Leaving work, Enfield Cycle Co, Hunt End, early 20th century.
LEFT: Advertisement for Royal Enfield Cycles made in Redditch. RIGHT:
The Redditch branch of the Alcester Cooperative Society, with staff on the
corner of Evesham Street and George Street.

LEFT: The Redditch Meat Co, pre-First World war. RIGHT: The Post Office, Church Road, in 1904. BELOW: The Parade (now Church Green West) in 1906.

ABOVE: *Redditch Indicator* illustration of shops and offices at the corner of Bates Hill and Church Green West, 1898. LEFT: Church Green East in 1900. RIGHT: Keir Hardie addressing a Labour demonstration, Redditch, 1906.

ABOVE: Redditch Artillery Volunteers on Easemore Road, 1907. BELOW:
Market Place, c1905.

ABOVE: Market Place, c1920. BELOW: The Market Place, Church Green and St Stephen's before 1914. Stalls were set up along the street during the 19th century and for many years of the 20th. Redditch has preserved its open air market.

ABOVE: Prospect Hill. A pre-First World War photograph from the belfry of St Stephen's. BELOW: Mount Pleasant, looking south in 1906, remarkably unchanged today.

ABOVE: Evesham Street from Church Green West c1910. The publisher of this and most other Edwardian views of Redditch traded from the second shop on the left. BELOW: Evesham Street shops 1913.

READING ROOM
FOR HEADLESS CROSS.

It is proposed to establish a Working Man's Room in this village, in which the Newspapers and Periodicals of the day will be placed ; and, in connection therewith, Lectures, Reading, Musical, and other Entertainments given.

TO-MORROW, AT SEVEN P.M.,

THERE WILL BE

A MUSICAL ENTERTAINMENT

IN

THE WESLEYAN SCHOOL ROOM.

Admission Free!   Males and Females both Invited ;
After which, further particulars will be given, and Members' names enrolled.

Sixpence per month, payable in advance, is proposed for the Fee, which will admit to the Reading Room, two Lectures, a Musical Entertainment, and Reading.   It is hoped, also, that in a short time there will be a well-furnished Library connected with the above room.

Your Co-operation is respectfully invited.

WILLIAM AVERY.

Headless Cross, Nov. 1, 1861.

W. T. HEMING, PRINTER.

Advertisement for one of William Avery's 'Entertainments', 1861.

REDDITCH RACES,
1865.

WHIT-MONDAY AND TUESDAY, JUNE 5th and 6th.

STEWARDS--
G. R. COLLIS, ESQ., AND E. HOLYOAKE, ESQ.

FIRST DAY.

The HEWELL (Selling) STAKES,
Of 2 Sovs. each, with 15 Sovs. added.

Two years old, 7st., three, 9st., four, 10st.5lb., five, 10st.12lb., six and aged, 11st.2lb. The winner to be Sold by Auction for £50; if entered to be sold for £40, allowed 5lbs., if for £30, 10lbs., and if for £20, 21lbs., the surplus (if any) to go to the Race Fund. Heats. About one mile.

THE INNKEEPERS' HANDICAP,
Of 5 Sovs. each, (1 forfeit to the fund,) with 20 Sovs. added.

Second horse to save his stake. The winner of any handicap value £50, after the publication of the weights, to carry 7lbs. extra. Heats. About one mile. Closed with 20 entries.

THE LADIES' PURSE,
Of 10 Sovs. added to a Sweepstakes of 2 Sovs. each.

Two years old, 6st., three, 8st., four, 9st.2lb., five, 9st.7lb., six and aged, 9st.9lb. Heats. About one mile.

A PONY RACE,
Of 5 Shillings each, with a Purse added.

For ponies not exceeding 13 hands high. Catch weight. Heats. About one mile.

SECOND DAY.

The SENSATION (Selling) STAKES.
Of 2 Sovs. each, with 15 Sovs. added.

Weights and Conditions same as the Hewell Selling Stakes, first day. Heats. About one mile.

THE STEWARDS' CUP,
Value 25 Guineas, (given by G. R. Collis and E. Holyoake, Esqs.) Added to a Sweepstakes of 3 Sovs. each.

Open to horses of all denominations. Second to save his stake. Not less than four horses will be allowed to start. Three years old, 7st.10lb., four, 9st.7lb., five, 10st., six and aged, 10st.9lb. About two miles and a quarter.

THE IPSLEY HANDICAP,
Of 5 Sovs. each, (2 forfeit to the fund,) with 40 Sovs. added.

Second horse to save his stake. Winner to pay 2 sovs. to the fund. The winner of any handicap value £50, after the publication of the weights, or of the Innkeepers' Handicap, to carry 7lbs. extra. About one mile. Closed with 23 entries.

A HANDICAP for BEATEN HORSES,
Of 1 Sov. each, with a Purse added.

To enter to the Secretary immediately after the Ipsley Handicap. Heats. About one mile.

Redditch Races (1865) were held on a small course off Beoley Road in the Arrow Valley.

LEFT: Bromsgrove Road in 1906 on one of E.A. Hodge's heraldic cards. The view is little changed today. RIGHT: Oswald Street, 1906. BELOW: Redditch Fair in 1907, and doubtless some familiar grand-paternal faces!

ABOVE: Lodge Road 1906. BELOW: Hewell Road, 1906.

ABOVE: Mount Pleasant, c1920. CENTRE: The first aeroplane to land in Redditch. A race from London to Manchester between Gustav Hamel and B.C. Hucks in 1913 used Beoley Road playing fields as a staging post. BELOW: The Redditch Town Band, photographed by A.H. Clarke, Redditch.

ABOVE: The Queen's Head, Bromsgrove Road, c1880. BELOW: The
Shakespeare Inn, Walford Street, c1910.

ABOVE: The Nevill Arms, Astwood Bank in 1914. BELOW: Lamb and Flag, Unicorn Hill c1920.

ABOVE: Recruiting Office for the First World War. BELOW: Peace Day,
Church Green, 19 July 1919.

119

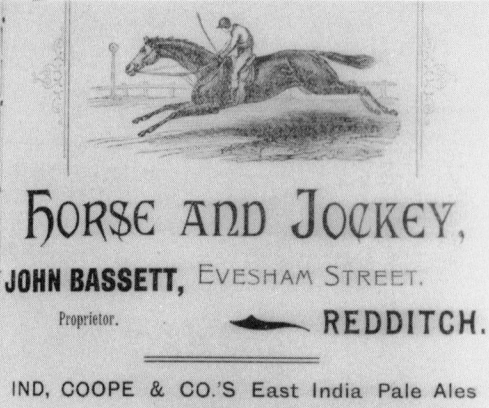

OPPOSITE ABOVE LEFT: Advertisement; Huins' Boots and Shoes 1901:
RIGHT and BELOW: from *The Needle District Almanack* 1901, and BELOW
RIGHT: in 1922.

ABOVE: Advertising in the 1920s. A Peakman Street wall with enamelled
signs which survived into the 1980s. BELOW: Abel Morrall Ltd, float for
Redditch Carnival, 1933.

ABOVE: Part of the Batchley Estate built by Redditch Council after the Second World War. BELOW: Holmwood, the palatial vicarage built by Canon H J. Newton. After a period as a convalescent home, it was used as the Headquarters of Redditch Development Corporation, 1964-85.

Old Town, New Town

Redditch emerged from the Second World War relatively unscathed. The few bombs which had fallen on the town had done little damage. This may have been a mixed blessing, for Redditch faced the future in 1945 with a serious housing problem. The population had reached 25,900 and was still growing. During the war, accommodation for essential workers had been provided by the Ministry of Labour in a hastily constructed Abbey Hostel, off the Birmingham Road. There was a waiting list of homeless people, which reached 1,000 by 1946. Added to these were the considerable number of Polish immigrants who decided to settle in the town. Redditch still suffered from the overcrowding and inadequate nature of much 19th century housing.

As a temporary measure, the Urban District Council built estates of prefabricated houses on Cedar Road, Dolphin Road and at Hunt End. Originally intended to last for ten years, most survived into the 1980s, and those on Dolphin Road appear permanent. These homes were only a stop-gap, and the Council solved its longer-term needs by the building of the Batchley Estate in the 1950s. It is fashionable to decry the large council estate today: when Batchley was built, it provided well built, sizeable, semi-detached houses with large gardens and landscaped open spaces for people who can never have known such delights. Batchley may well have been the only council estate anywhere with its own flock of Canada geese, previously the preserve of the stately home owner.

The Urban District Council attempted to tackle its responsibilities seriously, to the extent of commissioning Sir Patrick Abercrombie, the noted town planner, to produce a master plan for the development of the town. An imaginative plan, which envisaged a covered, traffic-free shopping area many years before other towns had them, was rejected by the Council in 1948. It was not possible for Redditch to divorce itself from its environment: though the town was in rural Worcestershire, the pressure for better housing was coming from the over-crowded and bomb-damaged conurbation of Birmingham and the West Midlands. There was fierce controversy in the 1950s over the part, if any, which Redditch should play in the solution of the over-spill needs of its mighty neighbour. Nonetheless there is a feeling that Redditch spent the twenty years after the end of the war waiting for something to happen.

The railway service went into a gentle decline, its virtual axeing by Dr Beeching in 1962 surprising no-one. The 'bus service, operating from a series of tin shacks on waste ground, remained deplorable. Redditch was connected with nowhere by what could be called a main road. It was possible to get wet and mud-splashed in the wholly inadequate shopping centre of Evesham Street: it was not possible to buy anything out of the ordinary. The great needle making families of the previous century had departed or died out: the industry had become the two huge and anonymous firms of Needle Industries and the British Needle Company. Redditch appeared to be without natural leaders and without ambition, until 21 January 1963, the fateful day on which the Minister of Housing and Local Government in the Macmillan Government, Sir Keith Joseph, announced that he intended to use the New Towns Act of 1946 to solve the problems of the West Midlands. Redditch was designated a New Town.

The post-war Labour Governments had used the Act to build a series of New Towns around London. Stevenage, Hatfield, Harlow, Crawley and Basildon were the first generation of such towns: they were joined a little later by towns in Scotland such as Cumbernauld and Livingston. By the 1960s the first flush of enthusiasm had died away. When Redditch was designated a New Town on 10 April 1964, it was one of a second generation which included Runcorn, Telford and Daventry, and which were different from their predecessors. The new idea was to expand an existing centre or centres by grafting the new on to the old and so, perhaps, avoid the disease known as New Town blues.

Redditch was to assist in solving the housing needs of the West Midland conurbation. The planners believed it was ideally situated near to, but physically separated from, the City of Birmingham. Despite the inadequacies of communications, water supply, sewage disposal and amenities, it was felt that Redditch offered an opportunity for rapid expansion. It would seem, too, that the agricultural land around the existing town would be inexpensive to buy and of little loss to the farming community. Wholesale redevelopment of a town centre, 'with little architectural character and with public buildings of no interest' (according to Pevsner) would not cause much difficulty. And the Redditch Urban District Council was a small local authority, run from a large house and several sheds, and unlikely to provide much resistance.

Progress following designation was extraordinarily rapid. The first Chairman of the Board of the New Town Corporation, Sir Edward Thompson, was appointed in 1964. He held office for ten years. Much of the success of the New Town may be explained by the fact that the Corporation enjoyed continuity of senior staff, having had only three Chairmen and three General Managers in the 21 years of its existence. The Chairmen were Sir Edward Thompson (1964-1974), James Chesshire (1974-1978) and Professor Denys Hinton (1978-1985). The General Managers were A.M. Grier (1964-1976), William C. Evans (1976-1979) and Norman More (1979-1985).

The Master Plan for Redditch New Town was produced by the firm of Wilson and Womersley, and was chiefly the work of Sir Hugh Wilson. His brief included the memorable advice that the Board did 'not want another bloody Cumbernauld in Redditch'. Sir Hugh lived until 1985, long enough to see that he had fulfilled his brief. The production of the Master Plan occupied most of 1965 and 1966. The wisdom of most of the original decisions has been justified. The town centre was to be redeveloped on its old site. St Stephen's Parish Church and the Church Green were to be preserved as a focal point for the integration of old and new. Most of the development was to occur east of the River Arrow, but was not to spoil the views across the valley from the old town towards rural Beoley and Ipsley. Everything possible was to be done to preserve existing trees and hedges.

The seriousness of this aim of the Corporation was shown by the publication of an Ecological Survey of the complete New Town area, and the most striking feature of the last twenty years has been the planting of new trees. The millionth was planted in the Town Centre in 1973. Mercifully, Sir Hugh decided there would be no high-rise building in this new town. Instead, housing would be provided in traditional terraces and squares, or in semi-detached or detached low-rise houses. Industrial estates were to be built within easy reach of residential areas. There was to be no through traffic in the areas where people lived, but each 'bead', as the planners called them, was to be linked with others, with the town centre, and with the outside world, by roads of motorway standards. Despite much criticism of the profligacy of such roads, the planners have been proved right. Redditch has a road system superior to any other town of its size. It does not have traffic jams, and is well planned to cope with the traffic demands of the 1990s. Only the imaginative, but expensive, public transport ideas of the original plan have failed to appear. After a public enquiry and a number of exhibitions and public meetings, the Master Plan was accepted and has been the basis for the massive changes of the past two decades.

For the first years of the work of the Corporation, much more seemed to be pulled down than erected. New housing did appear, at first in Greenlands and Woodrow, later in Matchborough and

Winyates, but it was easy to live in the older parts of Redditch and to be unaware of the rapid changes taking place elsewhere. Townspeople were aware that the former palatial vicarage of Canon Newton, called Holmwood, had been taken over as the headquarters of the Development Corporation. They saw that power over their lives was somewhat uneasily shared by the Councillors at the Mount Pleasant Council House, whom they elected, and the developers at Holmwood, whom they did not. They saw the bulldozers and earth-movers arrive, and suddenly realised that the lanes and tracks which had served the area for so long were to be replaced by dual carriageways and clover leaf junctions, which seemed to belong to California rather than to rural Worcestershire. Their sewage works off Studley Road vanished, being replaced by a huge modern complex out of sight and out of the designated area, at Spernal Ash in Warwickshire.

They saw a succession of Cabinet Ministers and lesser ministerial figures visit the town. Richard Crossman, Minister of Housing and Local Government in the Labour Government of 1964, seems not to have enjoyed his visit, being faced by critics of his own party who were describing Redditch as 'a bloody awful New Town'. Crossman, according to his diaries, agreed with them — but secretly. Both he, and they, have been proved wrong by events. Perhaps with greater significance, but without indiscreet diary references, Redditch was visited by two Prime Ministers, Edward Heath in 1973 and James Callaghan in 1976.

Much more important to the average Redditchian was what was happening to his town centre. For years, it seemed, old landmarks were disappearing and being replaced by the mud and inconvenience of building sites. In retrospect one must admire the remarkable way in which the life of Redditch Town Centre continued through nearly two decades of upheaval. The new was successfuly grafted onto the old, and life continued throughout. Appetites had been whetted in 1968 with the publication of the plans for the redeveloped town centre. An air-conditioned, traffic-free shopping area was envisaged, linked with a new 'bus and railway station (infelicitously called a transport inter-change), and with a number of multi-storey car parks. Redditch had never seen anything like it.

The most striking and controversial feature of Phase 1 was a central square, planted with palm trees! Remarks about taxpayers footing the bill for developers' extravagance were muted when it transpired that the trees were a gift to the town. Curiously, townspeople are now proud of this unique feature of their centre, which marks it out from all others. The planners wisely gave the shopping area the name of The Kingfisher Centre, thus preserving the town's links with a war-time destroyer, HMS *Kingfisher,* which the town adopted in 1941. The link has been revived by an association between the town and the present HMS *Kingfisher,* a fisheries protection vessel, whose home port is Gloucester, which may be described as Redditch's gateway to the sea. The Centre was completed in stages. Its facilities were widely advertised on television. The combination of large stores, small shops, an indoor and outdoor market, cafés and restaurants, and an exhibition centre and impromptu concert hall among the palm trees, has proved a remarkable success. People who, twenty years ago, would have dropped dead rather than go to dirty Redditch, now regularly visit the One Stop Shop.

Old-established shops and other buildings inevitably disappeared in the great rebuilding. Despite some emotional attachment to old Redditch, which meant little more than Redditch BC — before the Corporation — there was little of architectural merit worth preserving. The most notable victims were two huge nonconformist Chapels — Bates Hill Methodist Church of 1843 and Evesham Street Congregational Church of 1825. The opportunity was taken, at the initiative of the Congregationalists, to join with the Methodists to form a united body. With the Congregational Union with the Presbyterians, to form the United Reformed Church, came an opportunity for the development of an experiment in church unity which few towns can have experienced. With the active encouragement of the Bishop of Worcester, the Rt Rev Robin Woods, the Church of England became involved.

The vision of Rev Sydney Roberts of the URC and Rev Barrie Cooke of the Methodists gradually materialised, with the building of a Church and suite of church offices and rooms high above the Kingfisher Centre, in what came to be known unpronounceably as the Ecumenical Centre. The two congregations of Bates Hill and Evesham Street united their strengths as Trinity Church, Redditch, and the reality of creating a new town centre worshipping community fell to Rev David Marsden and Rev Frank Godfrey. Both Centre and Church fulfil a major need: thanks to the palm trees they are able to hold, with a real donkey, the most realistic Palm Sunday service anywhere in England. Trinity Church was opened in February 1976 by the Bishop of Worcester, the Chairman of the Methodist District and the Moderator of the United Reformed Church Hereford and Worcester Synod. Royal approval of the venture was given two years later when HRH Prince Philip, Duke of Edinburgh, spoke in Trinity Church to an invited audience.

At the same time as the town was seeing both upheaval and rebirth, the system of education in Redditch, as elsewhere in the country, was being dramatically restructured. Out went the tri-partite system, to be replaced in Redditch by comprehensive schools, with children transferring schools at nine and thirteen. The first sign of such changes came with the opening in 1971 of the Leys High School, to serve the south-eastern areas of the town. Close on its heels came the building of a flood of first and middle schools, and the change in status of Bridley Moor Secondary School and the former County High School into 13-18 coeducational comprehensives. The process was continued with the opening of St Augustine's Roman Catholic High School in Hunt End, and concluded with the opening in 1976 of Arrow Vale High School to serve the New Town areas east of the River Arrow. Both Arrow Vale and the Leys High Schools were provided with facilities for dual use, so that sports halls, squash courts, theatres and other areas might be used by the local community out of school hours. Major extensions were also made to the buildings and facilities of Redditch College of Further Education.

It had become apparent by the early 1980s that Redditch Development Corporation had produced a thriving, successful and attractive New Town. Remarkably, it is still possible to see trees and green fields from almost anywhere in the town. The attractive, rolling, wooded landscape of 18th century Worcestershire has been preserved, and the work of the landscape architects of the Corporation is beyond praise. This is less true of the architects of individual buildings, few of which lay any claim to distinction. The Corporation preserved and renovated the Palace Theatre, which retains all the cosy intimacy and velvet plush of a playhouse originally opened in 1913. The Kingfisher Centre is an excellent example of a functional building, but few would describe it as beautiful. The only two major buildings of the re-development which should pass the test of time as good architecture were not the work of the Development Corporation at all. The Public Library designed by the John Madin Group in the Market Place is both fine to look at and pleasant to use — a lasting tribute to an earlier librarian and historian of the town, Roy Vann. Further down Alcester Street, Redditch at last gained a Town Hall, a large and impressive brick building of some distinction, which may do something to give civic pride to a town which has suffered too long from a lack of it. It was opened in 1982 at a cost of £7,500,000.

If there are criticisms of what has happened in the past twenty years,the major omission must be the provision of a general hospital. The Smallwood Hospital of 1895 was inadequate when the town was designated a New Town in 1964. It became still more so with the withdrawal of casualty facilities after 5.00 pm each day. The inability of governments to find the money, and the deplorable, endless bickering between Bromsgrove and Redditch over the site of the new hospital have ensured that 70,000 people are still, in 1985, waiting for the arrival of a basic facility.

The work of the Development Corporation should have ended in 1982. For a variety of reasons its life was extended, firstly to 1984, and then to midsummer of 1985. On 15 May 1980 Redditch, at last, became a Borough with its own Mayor. The Charter Mayor was Councillor Ken Redfern. With the opening of the Town Hall two years later Redditch had come of age. The party of celebration was delayed until 5 July 1983 when, on a gloriously sunny day, Redditch was visited by HM Queen Elizabeth II. The first Royal visit since 1328, when Edward III visited Bordesley Abbey, saw the Queen greeted outside St Stephen's Church by the Lord Lieutenant of the County, and the Mayor of Redditch, Councillor Mrs Betty Passingham. The Queen toured the Kingfisher Centre and named the square containing the Paolozzi murals, Milward Square, in token of the town's indebtedness to the needle industry. The familiar walk-about took Her Majesty through Royal Square and to the Town Hall for lunch. Afterwards she declared open the National Needle Museum in the restored Forge Mill, signalling the restart of the water wheel and the needle scouring beds, which had lain silent since Mr Jakeman put his coat on and locked the door in 1958. He was there to show the Queen how needles should be scoured. Finally the Queen visited the ultra-modern new town factory of Hymatic Engineering Limited.

That crowded, happy, sunlit day of 1983, with thousands of Redditch people, from old town and new, may serve as the end of our story. Well over two thousand years have passed since some unknown Britons dug The Mount at Beoley or trod the Ridge Way. Romans came and went. Saxons came and settled. The people of Ipsley tilled their fields under the orders of the Huband family for seven hundred years. The Cistercians came, builded, prayed, grew rich and were dissolved. Needle makers came and prospered and have been replaced by other engineers with other remarkable skills. The Corporation has come and gone, leaving behind a remarkable modern creation. They are but the last in a series of people and organisations who have left their mark on the town of Redditch.

The extensive view from The Mount, Beoley.

127

In Praise of Redditch Town

Of all the towns on England's ground,
Few like Redditch are to be found:
For situation, money and trade,
A finer village was never made.

The houses are elegant and fine,
With windows sash't, O how they shine;
With gravel walks and a pleasant green,
A finer village was never seen.

The girls are numerous and very fair;
In dress few with them can compare;
And if abroad they chance to roam,
They never leave their best at home.

The publics find a ready sale
For Birmingham beer, likewise for ale;
The pointer lads regard no sorrow,
And never provide for the morrow.

The gentlemen have a fine rule
And did erect a Sunday School,
A charity right good I am sure,
To teach the children of the poor.

John Hollis of Tardebigge c1820

Sunset on Redditch past and present. Photograph by Michael L. Wojczynski (1985), showing the present day sky-line and the history of the town from Bordesley Abbey to the New Town.

Bibliography

General

Nash, T.R.	*History and Antiquities of Worcestershire* (2 vols 1781-2)
Dugdale, William	*History of Warwickshire* (1661)
Habington, Thomas	*A Survey of Worcestershire* (2 vols ed Amphlett J. 1893)
Rolt, L.T.C.	*Worcestershire* (1949)
Fraser, Maxwell	*Companion into Worcestershire* (1949)
Houghton, F.T.S.	*Worcestershire — The Little Guides Series* (1952)
Lees Milne, J.	*Shell Guide to Worcestershire* (1964)
Pevsner, Nikolaus	*The Buildings of England — Worcestershire* (1968)
Leatherbarrow, J.S.	*Worcestershire* (1974)

Victoria County History of Worcestershire (1901-24 Reprinted 1971)
Victoria County History of Warwickshire (1904-1969)

Histories of Redditch

Avery, William	*Old Redditch* (1887)
Rollins, J.G.	*A History of Redditch* (1984)
Land, Neville	*The History of Redditch and the Locality* (1985)
Anstis, G.M.	*The History of Redditch New Town (1964-1985)* (1985)

Novel

Clews, Roy	*Young Jethro* (1975)

Early History

	Worcestershire Archaeology Newsletters (1967-1985)
	The Archaeology of Redditch New Town Parts 1 and 2 (1969-70)
Duignan, W.H.	*Worcestershire Place Names* (1905)
Mawer, A. and Stenton, F.M.	*The Place Names of Worcestershire* (1927)
Dickins, Margaret	*A Thousand Years in Tardebigge* (1931)
	Domesday Book re-print *Worcestershire* (1982)

Bordesley Abbey

Knowles, D.	*The Monastic Order in England* (2nd ed 1963)
Knowles D. & Hadcock, R.N.	*Medieval Religious Houses of England and Wales.* (1971)
Woodward, J.M.	*The History of Bordesley Abbey* (1866)
Andrews, F.B.	*Memorials of Old Worcestershire* (1912)
Rahtz, P. & Hirst, S.M.	*Bordesley Abbey, Redditch*
Rahtz, P. & Hirst, Susan	*Bordesley Abbey, Redditch.* British Archaeological Report 23 (1976)
Hirst, S.M., Walsh, D.A. Wright, S.M.	*Bordesley Abbey, Redditch II* British Archaeology Report 111 *(1983)*

The Sheldons of Beoley

	The Parish Church of St. Leonard, Beoley Church Guide (1972)
Barnard, E.A.B.	*The Sheldons* (1936)
	The Weavers of Sheldon Tapestries (1928)
Wace, A.S.B.	*The Sheldon Tapestries* (1928)
Humphreys, John	*The Sheldon Tapestry Maps of Worcestershire* Transactions of the Birmingham Archaeological Society (1919)

Needlemaking

Dickens, Charles	*Household Words* (1852)
Morrall, M.T.	*History and Description of Needlemaking* (2nd ed 1854)
Morrall, T.M.	*The Needle* (1857)
Timmins S. ed	*Birmingham and Midland Hardware District* (1866 reprinted 1967)
Heming, W.T.	*The Needle District Almanack and Trades Directory for Redditch and Neighbourhood (1866-1936)*
	The Needle Region and its Resources (1877)
Japp, Alexander Hay	*Industrial Curiosities* (1877)
Morrall, A.E.	*A Short Description of Needlemaking* (1886)
Shrimpton, William (compiler)	*Notes on a decayed needle land* (1897)
Milward, Henry & Sons	*Needlemaking — a guide through Washford Mills* (1898)
Guise, H.	*Needles, the History and Romance of an Industry* (1936)
Hardy, S.M.	*An Account of the Needle Industry up to the beginning of the Factory System* (unpublished M Comm Thesis University of Birmingham 1940)
White, George	*Early Needlemaking* (Transactions of the Newcomen Society 1941)
Webb, B.D.	*The Needle Industry of the Redditch Region* (unpublished Thesis. University of Southampton 1960)
Nokes, B.C.G.	*John English of Feckenham, Needlemanufacturer* (Business History 1969)
Rollins, J.G.	*The Needle Mills (1970)*
Jones, S.R.H.	*The Rise of the Factory System in the British Needle Industry 1820-1865)* (Unpublished presentation 1972)
	Development of Needle Manufacturing in the West Midlands before 1750 (Economic History Review 1978)
	John English and Co., Feckenham (Unpublished Ph D Thesis University of London 1980)
Booth, D.T.N.	*Warwickshire Watermills* (1978)
Alcester & District Local History Society	*The Industrial Archaeology of the Lower Arrow Valley, Warwickshire* (1979)
	Needlemakers and Needlemaking of the Alcester, Sambourne and Studley Area (1981)
Rollins, J.G.	*Needlemaking* (1981)
Luty, John	*Needlemaking and the Forge Mill*
Needle Industries Ltd *The History of the Needle*	
Nash, L.	*The Development of Redditch through the Needle Trade* (Unpublished thesis)

Redditch in the Early Modern Period

Small, K.A.	*Ipsley Court and the Huband Family* (1980)
Mabey, Margaret	*The Windsors of Hewell* (1981)
	Worcester Records - Sessions Rolls Part 1 and 2 (1899)
Drake, Daphne	*Bordesley Hall* (1956)
Monk, Joseph	*Itinerary of Redditch* (1776)
	An Act for building a chapel in the Hamlet of Redditch in the Parish of Tardebigge, in the Counties of Worcester and Warwick (1805)

Minney, T. Brendan	*Reddite Deo - Catholic Life from the foundation of Bordesley Abbey to that of Mount Carmel*
Smith, R.C.S.	*A study of the Old Poor Law: the parish of Ipsley, Warwicks 1797-1804*

The Nineteenth Century

Bentley's History, Guide and Directory of . . . the manufacturing town of Redditch (1835)

Renshaw, Ann	*The Development of Redditch in the Nineteenth Century* (Unpublished thesis)
Bolt, R.M.	*The Growth and Functions of Redditch* (unpublished BA Thesis. University of Birmingham 1957)
Vann, Roy	*A Short History of Redditch Parish Church* (1955)
Noake, John	*The Rambler in Worcestershire* (2 Vols 1851)
	Noake's Guide to Worcestershire (1868)
Page, Herbert	*2nd Annual Report on the Sanitary Condition of the Urban Sanitary Authority of Redditch for the year ending 31 December 1875 (1876)*
	Minute Books of the Bromsgrove Poor Law Union (1836-)
Avery, William	*In Memoriam - William Avery J.P.* (1899)
	Old Redditch (1887)
	Memorial Volumes 1-8
Rollins, J.G.	*Deposit of Documents - Worcester County Record Office Accession No 9159*
	The Redditch Indicator, 1859-

Transport

Hadfield, Charles	*British Canals - an illustrated History (4th ed 1973)*
	Canals of the West Midlands
Christiansen, Rex	*A Regional History of the Railways of Great Britain* Vol 7 *The West Midlands* (Revised edition 1983) Vol 13 *Thames and Severn* (1981)
Morgan, David ed	*The Redditch Railways 1859-1979* (1979)
Morgan, David ed	*Redditch Railways revisited* (1983)
Jarvis, Philip K.	*Steam on the Birmingham - Gloucester Loop* (1985)
Redditch New Town	*Planning Proposals - Redditch New Town* (1966)
Fincher, F.	*Redditch Ecological Survey* (1966)

Redditch Public Library has an excellent collection of local history material and good conditions for its study — made still better by the courtesy and helpfulness of the staff.

I have found the staff of the County Record Office at St Helen's, Worcester, extremely obliging in explaining and finding their considerable Redditch collection of documents and printed material.

Index

ENDPAPERS: 17th century Sheldon tapestry map of Worcestershire and Warwickshire (detail). The home of the Sheldons at Beoley is just above centre on the right hand edge. (Reproduced by courtesy of the Board of Trustees of the Victoria and Albert Museum)

Subscribers

Presentation Copies

1 **The Borough of Redditch**
2 **Hereford and Worcester County Council**
3 **Redditch Library**
4 **Councillor A.F. Price**
5 **Roy Vann**

6 Ralph Richardson
7 Clive and Carolyn Birch
8 Joan Richardson
9 Martin Richardson
10 J.W. Turnbull
11
13 G. Reddish
14 Mr & Mrs W.G. Thomas
15 Raymond Halmshaw
16 John D. Wall
17 Alwymn G. Griffiths
18 Anne Bradley
19 M.F. Beckham
20 Noel Pritchard
21 David Adshead
22 Penny Adams
23 Mark Taylor
24 Stanley Taylor
25 Moatfield Middle School
26 Miss E.H. Vickerton
27 Philip Jarvis
28 M.V. White
29
32 John F. Smith
33 Geoffrey John Gough
34 Mrs Margaret Smith
35 R.T. Maries
36 Mrs Mona Smith
37 D.C. Waddy
38 Mr & Mrs R.D. Cruise
39 Victoria & Albert Museum
40 London Guildhall Library
41 John Slater
42 John A. Harley
43 D.J. Tilsley
44 Birmingham Reference Library
45 Malcolm L. Hall
46 Mrs S. Gibbons
47 R.D. Orford
48 Mrs J.E. Brooks
49 Wilfred Carpenter
50 Mrs J. Parker
51 B. Hart
52 Mrs M. Green
53 S.W. Freeman
54 Michael G.M. Kenny
55 G. Reddish
56 Mrs C.M. Allured
57 Miss S. Harvey
58 Mrs C. Tingle
59 P.T.G. Woollacott
60 John M. Allinson
61 J.B. Chandler
62 I.D. Turner ABI.D.
63 D.C. Pierson
64 Mrs J.M. Turk
65 F. Russell
66 Roy Banks
67 L.V.J. Blumfield
68 Mrs Helen Cartwright

69 N. Neasom
70 Miss M.A. Lake
71 C.G. Stallard
72 Mrs P.K. Wrighton
73 Mrs J. Turner
74 D.S. Parker
75 H.A. Craig
76 Mrs Jean Birch
77 G. Moore
78 G. Johnson
79 Mrs P.M. Dixon
80 Mrs Elizabeth Atkins
81 Mrs Joan Gadd
82 Mr & Mrs J.L. Moss
83 Mrs M. Jay
84 A. Lee
85 R.H. Harris
86 Jean Alker
87 Mrs J. Bonham
88 Mr & Mrs N. Land
89 W.A. Smith
90 B. Byng
91 R.J. Saunders
92 Dr B. Foyle
93 Miss C. Malcolmson
94 Mr & Mrs S.W. Sole
95 Mrs Penelope J. Bradley
96 J.M. Small
97 Ian Hayes
98 Miss B.J. Wiggett
99 P.G. Beckhelling
100 R.J. Howes
101 Mrs M.L. Gorton
102 A.J. Hall
103 The Bishop of Bristol the Rt Rev Barry Rogerson
104 Mr & Mrs A.W. Docker
105 Ken Mallam
106 Ruth Dolan
107 Mrs Helen Howard
108 B. Wright
109 J.W. Shakles
110 G.H. Quiney
111 Janet Hollington
112 Elizabeth Heneghan
113 Pamela J. Young

114 Richard A. Churchley
115 Mr & Mrs W.G. Thomas
116 Martyn Cutmore
117 Roger Satterthwaite
118 Mrs C.E. Watson
119 Mrs S. Miles
120 Mrs W. Savage
121 P. Robinson
122 Robin Whittaker
123
124 Mrs J.H. Cottrill
125 Mrs Marilyn Lloyd
126 J.E. Wren
127 Mrs Mary Volrath
128 Mrs J.M. Jarratt
129 Mrs F.M. Hopkins
130 V.J. Dudley
131 Mrs Jean West
132 Mrs Peggy Helme
133 Mrs Bettina Whitford
134 Mr & Mrs L. Cox
135 Charles S. Witherington-Perkins
136 Leonard G. Baker
137 Enid Tonkiss
138 Mrs Barbara Waller
139 J.E. Shufflebotham
140 Norman W. Thomas
141 Mrs Kathleen
142 Mary Paterson
143 Eileen Hill
144 Winifred Savery
145 David R. Morgan
146 Mr & Mrs R.J. Pooler
147 K.L. Smith
148 Margot Nash
149 J.B. Sampson
150 Mr & Mrs Mikkelsen
151 Mr & Mrs A. Hodges
152 Woodrow First School
153 Mrs A.C. Ball
154 J.L.M. Normansell
155 N.M. Whitehead
156 J. Williamson
157 Kerwood & Company
158 R.J. Swann
159 Mrs J.M. Smith
160 Sheila J. Darby

161 Adrian Burley
162 Dorothy Carlton
163 Irma J. Hull
164 Philip Davis
165 Mrs M.M. Saunders
166 G.V. & D. Crow
167 Rev & Mrs D. Bosworth
168 Mrs J.M. Richardson
169 Arthur & Doreen Price
170 Mrs M. Jones
171 Philip A. Smith
172 R. Sukevics
173 Elsie Haden
174 Mrs N. Owen
175 Mrs D.M. Oscroft
176 G.D. Watson
177 A.D. Bradbury
178 David McNally
179 J.C.W. Hart
180 Mrs Shirley Jones
181 George Donald Pickering
182 A. McNally
183 H.L. Morgan
184 D.T. Harrison
185 Mrs Mary Wilson
186 Miss Penny Wilson
187 Tony Carr
188 Mr & Mrs L. Tomlinson
189 Mary & Brian Foster
190 Friends of Auxerre
191 Canon & Mrs J.R. Gathercole
192
193 Mrs H.I. Evans
194 I.D. Hillman
195 R.A. Sanderson
196 Carol Rose
197 John Wagstaff
198 G.B. Seddon
199 Roy T. Vickers
200 Mrs P. Dight
201 Mrs P. Saunders
202 A.S. Freeman
203 Borough of Redditch
204 Prof & Mrs J.B. Lloyd
205 Borough of Redditch
206 Mrs G. Stone
207 Steven Last
208 Miss E.A. Morris
209 Lindsay Bowman
210
211 V.S. & K.W. Barber
212 R.N. Davis
213 M.B. Davis
214 The Woodrush High School
215 Derek J. Hooker
216 Michael L. Wojczynski
217 Michael S. Darby
218 Ironbridge Gorge Museum
219 Mrs J. Beard
220 Mrs H. Johnson
221 Susan Tatlow

222 Paul Wilde
223 Mrs Anne Heath
224 John Henney
225 Mrs H.M. Armitage
226 Dominic Clarke
227 M.J. Hale
228 Frederick A. Stephens
229 Dr T. Fryers
230 Basil Gardner
231 T.A. Palmer
232 Lodge Farm Middle School
233
234 Mrs Meriel Hayes
235
236 T. Blount
237
238 J. Battle-Welch
239
240 Michael John Dunham
241 K. Dewhurst
242 Mrs J. Dewhurst
243
244 Mrs G.M. Moore
245
249 Arrow Vale High School
250
254 Mr & Mrs K. Mallam
255 R.F. Batts
256 Mrs Peggy Dufficey
257 Mr & Mrs H. Guise
258 Mr & Mrs R.W. Pennells
259 Mrs J. Patterson
260 Mrs G. Spires
261 Mr & Mrs A.J. Dean
262 Mr & Mrs A.T. Kain
263 M et Mme J.R. Renaudin
264 Jack Millward
265 Mrs A. Garman
266 Mrs K. Buckley
267 Clive Robinson
268 Mr & Mrs P. Howitt
269 Mrs J.V. Palmer
270 R. Vann
271 Beresford George Green
272 Kevin John Hurley
273 Marjorie Harker
274 Mr & Mrs E. Evans
275 Stuart & Sylvia North
276 George McCarthy
277 F.E. Chettle
278 G.P. Godfrey
279 J.B. Coleman
280 Frank Pattison
281 Ken Pattison
282 Michael Boxall
283 Trevor Sydney Wells
284 J.H. Hutchinson
285 Ceinwen H. Rice
286 D.H. Phipps & J.H. Phipps

287 M.J. Woodfield
288 J.R. Hobbs
289 Ken & Pat Randall
290 L. Watson
291 G.J. Gough
292 T.J. Bownes
293 C.H. Taylor
294 Brian Adams
295 Nigel & Karen Topley
296 S.D. Orford
297 Brian Yeomans
298 T. Thomas
299 T.S. Birkett
300 M. Broomfield
301 J.S. Sivyer
302 John Henry Bladon
303 Ronald Perrins
304 Margaret A. Edgar
305 Richard M. Simmons
306 John Bonaker
307 Susan Laight
308 Nicholas & Frances Taylor
309 Grace & John Tongue
310 Mark & Lydia Stephens
311 Anthony Kerr Strong
312 Les & Jill Evans
313 H. Hickman
314 Carole Peake
315 Gordon Moberley
316 Jill Smith
317 Mrs Deborah Mahony
318 Mrs V.A. George
319 Malcolm & Angela Haden
320 Dr J.W. Hopton
321 Peter Bonsall
322 Brian J. Bickley
323 Rosalind Mary Harding
324 Miss G.E. Hall
325 Rosemary Reeves
326 Mayrose Warner
327 Graham Simpson
328 Hereford & Worcester
378 County Council
379 Reverend S.W. Rose
380 I.K. Whitford
381 James Henry Brown
382 Edgar Jones
383 Peter J. Brown
384 A.D. Khosla
385 Arrowcrest First School
386 Phyllis Williams
387 Christine Tapson
388 Mr & Mrs A.A. Traves
389 Miss V.M. Ramsey
390 John Hirons
391 C. Wheeler
392 Mrs G.E. Slade
393 A.A. Upton
394 Brian Stallard
395 Mrs M. Sayers

396 John Gines
397 A.E. Young
398 S.J. Baird
399 W.F. Norton
400 Kevin Moore
401 Joan Jenkins
402 P. Toolan
403 B. Leech
404 David Ian Foulkes
405 Reginald Dennis Barley
406 D.L. Clarke
407 Walter & Betty Stranz
408 Patricia K. Wilson
409 David Watton
410 Andrew Turner
411
412 Mrs Shelley Forman
413 G. Malpass
414 J.M. Small
415 Eric Forth MP
416 Diana Bishop
417 Mrs Valerie Arnold
418 John Edwin Dickens
419 Mrs Carole Hough
420 I.T. Lyall
421 W.A. Bradley
422 P.R. Wilson
423 Stanley A. Budd
424 Mr & Mrs R. Dunkley
425 S.F.H. Johnson
426 Godfrey Knight
427 George Langston
428 R.M. Williams
429 G. Pye
430 Mrs Margaret Gopsill
431 R.J. Smith
432 Andy & Mandy Hardwick
433 Mr & Mrs G.W. Firth
434 Gilbert Willows
435 Miss C.M. Burrell
436 Mrs Joyce M. Towers
437 Raymond Hutchinson
438 The Reverend Barrie G. Cooke
439 Graham Allnatt
440 Bridley Moor High School
441 J.J. Smith
442 Mrs E.M. Cardwell
443 Mr & Mrs H. Potter
444 G. Kingston
445 Mrs K.M. Waud
446 F.I. Blencowe
447
448 Mrs M. Eccles
449 Mrs C.M. Partridge
450
451 E.V. McEnery
452 Redditch College Library
453 Mrs D. Cund

454 Mrs G. Moore
455 Mr & Mrs W.A. Baker
456 M.R. French
457
458 P.H. Riman
459
461 C.E. Ellis
462 John C.W. Hart
463 St Stephen's Middle
464 School
465 Councillor C.J. Cheetham
466 William C. Evans
467 Graham Faulkner
468 E. Gwynn Evans
469 E. Ruth C. Jackson
470 Walter A. Detheridge
471 R. Custerson
472 Lorna Matthews
473 Barbara J. Drain
474 D.A. Yapp
475 Mrs J. Warby
476 Mr & Mrs D.A.J. Stanley
477 Mr & Mrs W.E. Thompson
478 Esme A. Hayston
479 Miss Julie Maries
480
482 Mr & Mrs J. Greenacre
483 Michael Ann Dennis
484 Mr & Mrs W.J. Hawkes
485
486 R. Harris
487
489 R.F. Allen
490 D.D. George
491 Mrs D.M. Phelps
492 Icknield First School Library
493 Ridgeway Middle School
494 G. & R.I. Bulmer – Kirby
495 Janet Ann Surman
496 Mrs S.J. Sage
497 Maurice Willows
498 Brendan Hanrahan, Editor, Redditch Advertiser/Indicator
499 Mrs M.E. Harley
500 Mrs Y.D. Perring
501 K.D. Jubb
502 Rev J.W. Pearson
503 F.H. Postlethwaite
504
511 Miss V.J. Cole
512
513 Abbey High School
514 Rev & Mrs Lindsay Bowman
515 Rev & Mrs Frank Godfrey

Remaining names unlisted

136

ON·COFELD

YARDLEY
COLE

YARNTON

MOV

ARR·CHA
PERIHALL
ASTON
DVDSON

HAMSTED HOVNDSWORTH
BROMICHAM EDGBASTON

HAR

SANDWALL

WEST·BRAMWICH
SMETHICKE
WARTLEY
HALL

OLDBVRY
CHA

TIPTON

DVDLEY
CAS
DVDLEY
ROWLEY

RVSSELS
HAL

SEDGELEY